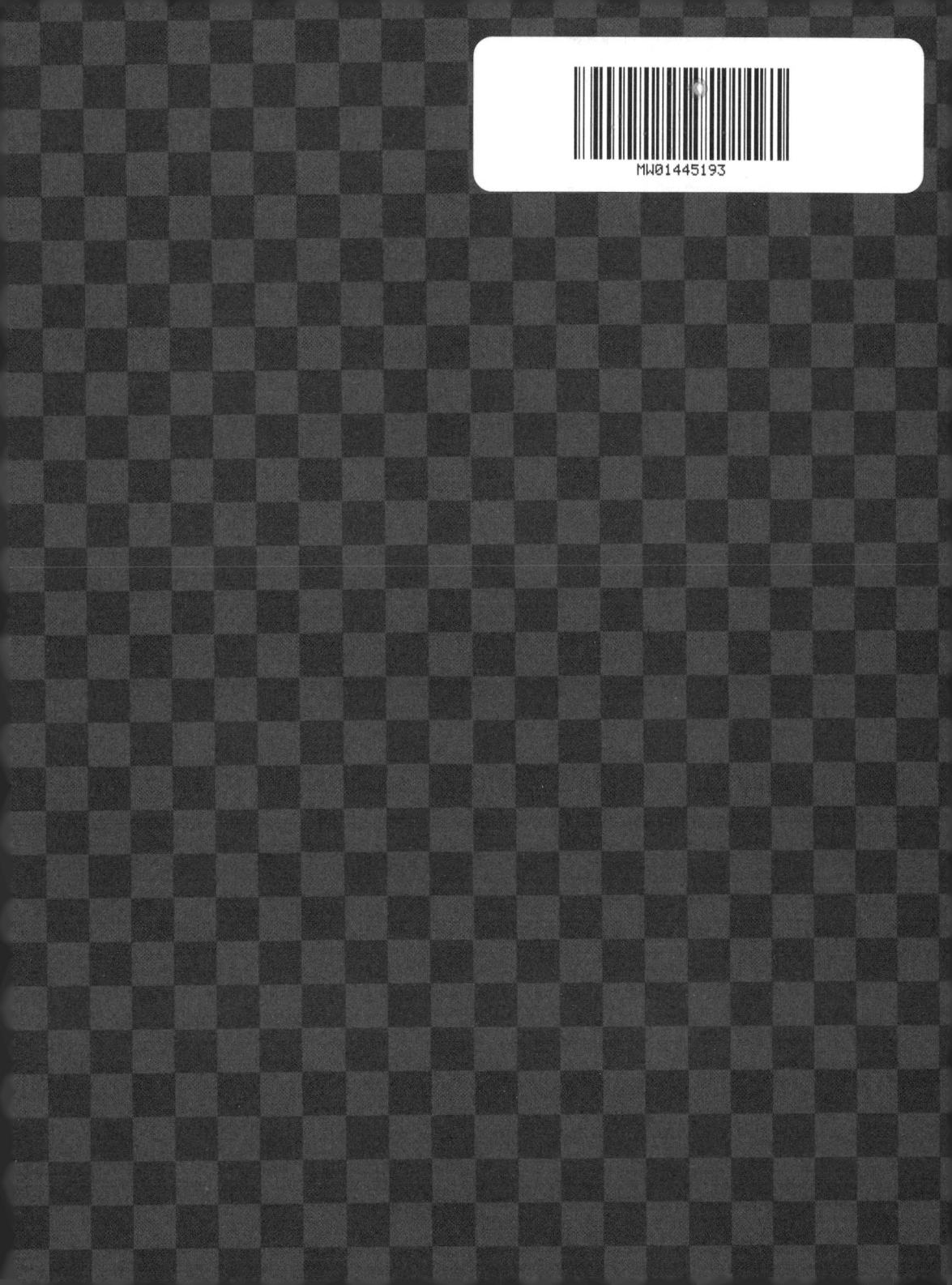

A Little *of* What You Fancy

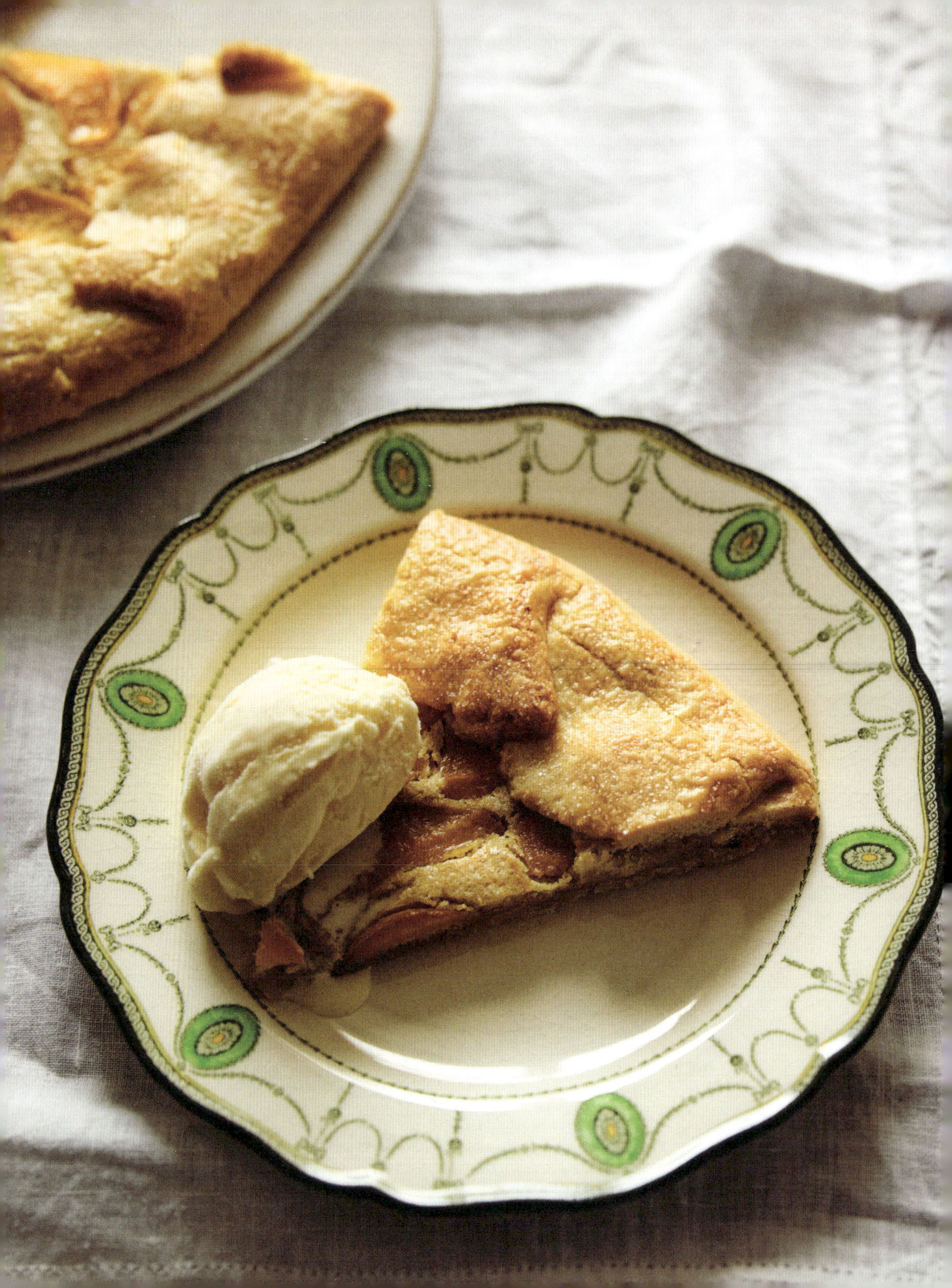

A Little *of* What You Fancy

Irresistible Small-Batch Bakes

DEE OMOLE

Quadrille

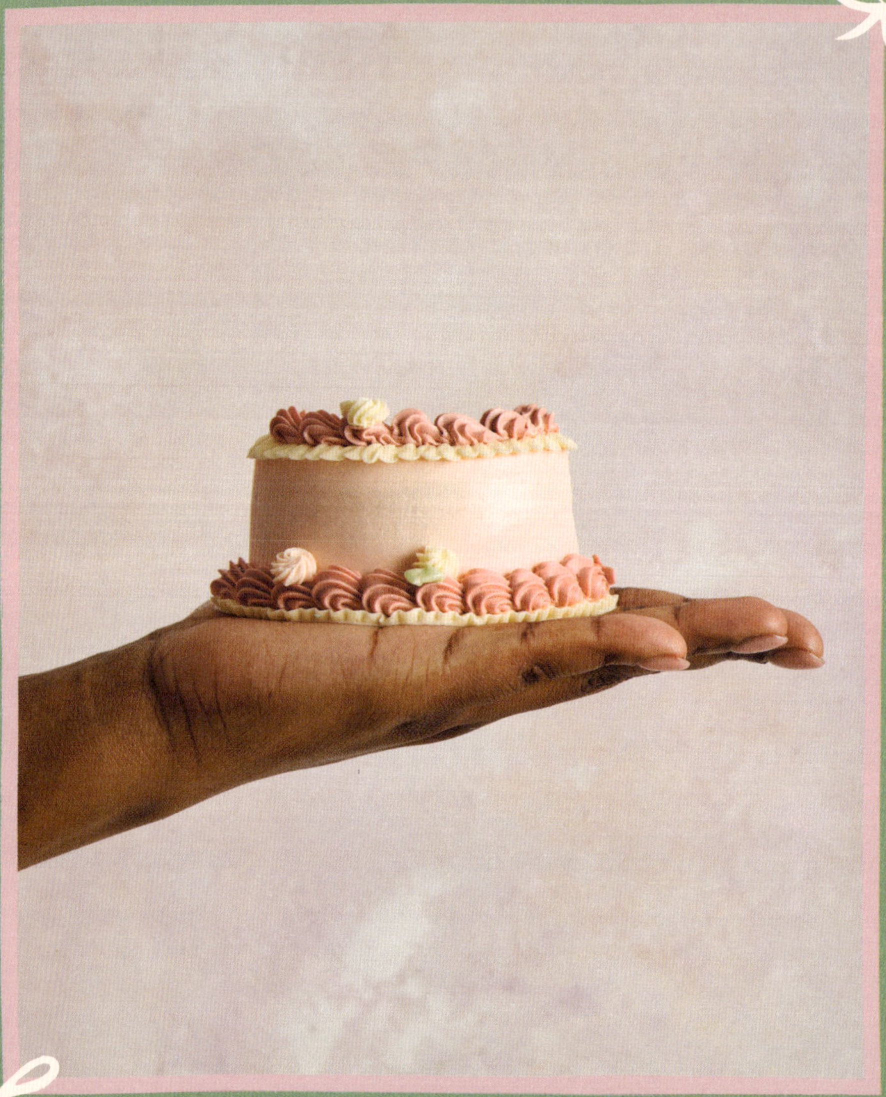

| Introduction | Equipment List | Tips & Tricks |
| 7 | 10 | 12 |

Basics 15

Cakes 33

Cookies & Biscuits 63

Desserts 79

Pastries 99

| About the Author | Acknowledgements | Index |
| 118 | 120 | 122 |

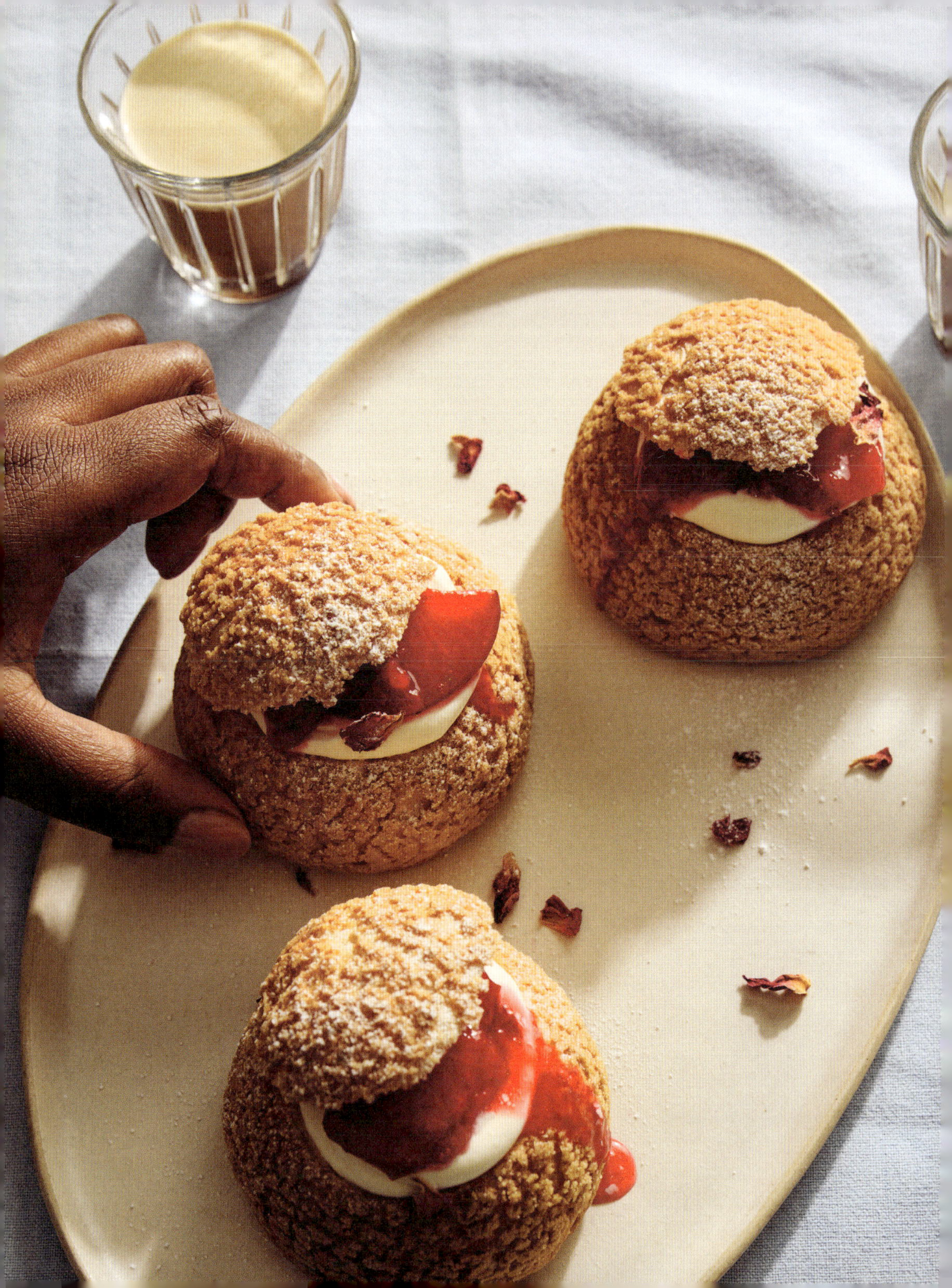

INTRODUCTION

This is very exciting and surreal to be writing an introduction to my first-ever published book! It has been an aspiration of mine and although younger me thought I'd have a book by 21 (not sure why that age), I truly believe everything happens for a reason when it's supposed to, so here I am at 29 with a published book.

So where did this all start? My first memories of baking are at around six years old with my mum. The first recipe I learnt, which I have included in this book, was a traditional Madeira-style vanilla cake (page 36). It was a great way to start baking as it is a basic recipe, which is very hard to mess up. Growing up in a Nigerian household, food has always been important to my family and so the years after learning that very first recipe I spent watching a variety of cooking and baking shows. One of my earliest memories of a cooking show was *Ready Steady Cook*. It was always fun to watch. The chefs had to create dishes in a matter of minutes based on ingredients they were presented with. It was very creative and made me think of what dishes I would create myself if I was on the show (at six years old, haha!). There were, of course, other cooking shows, and chefs with their own TV programmes like Gary Rhodes, Rick Stein and Nigella Lawson, but one of the reasons *Ready, Steady, Cook* became a firm favourite was Ainsley Harriott. He was the first black person I remember who was cooking and hosting a TV cookery show, which was a big thing for six-year-old me, and he's obviously incredibly talented and funny.

I continued to watch and expand my love of food and cooking by watching TV programmes such as *Barefoot Contessa*, which made me want a bakery in the Hamptons, and *Cake Boss*, which had a bit of everything and frankly had my whole family hooked. Heston Blumenthal also helped expand my imagination on what's possible with food. Another core memory I have of cooking shows was watching Lorraine Pascale for the first time, which really excited me as she had her own TV programme as well as cookbooks. Although I already thought anything was possible this was physical representation, which inspired me even more.

I've known I've always wanted a career in food. When I was younger, I even had the aspiration of having a restaurant and getting a Michelin star. Never say never, but over the years doing lots of work experience and agency work in restaurants I found it quite overwhelming, so I decided to work in calmer environments, such as bakeries and coffee shops. Even though it was still a lot of work and was overwhelming at times, I preferred it to restaurants. Although not all my experiences were amazing, the best one and the one that has stuck with me was at Konditor (previously known as Konditor & Cook).

Back in 2015, I had finished university for that year and was working at John Lewis at the weekends so my weekdays during that summer were free. I did an eight-week work experience at Konditor, which was broken up into four weeks of baking and four weeks of cake decorating. I learnt so much during those eight weeks and it gave me a great foundation for baking, especially decorating skills that I still use today. It has made me a lifelong fan of Konditor, especially their noisette cake, which I still order every year for my birthday. I developed my skills over the years through various work experiences, experimenting and trial and error by watching YouTube videos and practising designs and techniques on my family members' birthday cakes. With three sisters plus my mum, dad and other family members I always had opportunities to try new methods and designs.

So where did the Dee's Basement name come from, you may ask? For those who don't know me my full name is Adeola, and my nickname is Dee. Back in 2011, while at school, I wanted to create a blog where I could document my baking journey and share fun recipes; however, I needed a name. I wanted to include my nickname in the title to make it more personal – something like Dee's Space, but that sounded boring. My older sister helped and came up with Dee's Basement, which I liked and I ended up using it. I stopped blogging in 2017 but still had the name and thought it would be a great business name for when I started taking orders beyond family and friends.

I studied Business Management with Entrepreneurship at the University of Westminster and my final-year project was to create an actual business, so I used Dee's Basement as my business name. Once I graduated, I kept the name and business, and it became a side hustle while I was working in bakeries and coffee shops. Although I would have loved to have gone full-time with the business, my orders weren't consistent enough. I would send out hundreds of emails to brands offering samples and pitching ideas for catering, projects, etc. Although I only heard back from maybe 10 per cent of the emails I sent and some said yes just for the free samples, it was still a good way of getting the Dee's Basement name out there, especially as I didn't have a big social media presence.

Fast forward to 2020, I had just left my job as head baker at a coffee shop where I'd been for one and a half years and I decided that I was ready to go back and try working in a professional kitchen again within a restaurant. Not as work experience or agency work but a proper job as a commis pastry chef. This was in March 2020 so I think you know what's coming next. Covid! Although it was very early days here in the UK no one knew what was going on and I hadn't started my job yet. On my first day, it was the quickest bus journey of my life as the roads were very quiet. I turned up and saw my manager who was surprised to see me. He then proceeded to tell me that I was supposed to have been told not to come in as they had let go of all new staff and half of the kitchen, including me. My manager felt bad, especially as I had come in for my shift, so he gave me money out of his own pocket. He honestly didn't have to but that gesture meant a lot; a shout-out to Ernest!

The following week, the UK went into lockdown and I moved to my parents' house, which was outside London, thinking it would be just a couple weeks or months. My older sister encouraged me to do more baking, especially things I hadn't made before. By May, after baking banana breads and doing one too many TikTok dances, I started thinking of postal desserts, and I went full-time with Dee's Basement. I was posting all the baking I was doing for fun as well as sharing recipe videos on Instagram and TikTok. The Black Lives Matter movement was also very active at this time so a lot of people were sharing black-owned businesses and creators and I was also getting included in articles which increased brand awareness.

I began with postal cookies, which became popular, taking over my parent's kitchen and then also launched message traybakes. There were definitely teething issues figuring out packaging and sorting out postal logistics and delays, but that was all trial and error and I learnt a lot during that time. I was also doing a lot of brand mailers and orders including an order for 3,000 biscuits, which involved my whole family. They never let me forget this. Postal deliveries were doing well, but I wanted something completely unique to Dee's Basement, so after experimenting I launched chocolate-covered madeleines in November 2020 in cute designs including the cherries and edible flower designs (pages 46 and 47) I still do today. I continued to experiment with different postal desserts then events slowly started coming back, which meant more catering jobs and weddings. I moved into my own studio space in East London. This was a gamechanger and helped separate work from home. I've been fortunate and blessed to be self-employed since losing my job in 2020 and work with great brands and generally have amazing customers.

When I began baking and using cookbooks for basics and inspiration and baking more independently as I got older, the recipes made me nervous as they would use eight or nine eggs. This is a lot and is quite intimidating, especially when I'd never baked the recipe before, so I messed up the recipes and ended up wasting lots of eggs, plus whatever other ingredients I'd used. Of course, I could halve the recipe from time to time but that left room for error if I'd accidentally calculated something wrong or the number was an odd number so couldn't be divided evenly like a five-egg recipe, so I'd have to estimate, which isn't ideal in baking as you need to be quite accurate. That's why it was really important for this book to have simpler recipes, which are friendly for beginners or those who don't want to bake too much. You can of course easily double or triple the recipe quantities without having to worry about accuracy and wastage. Ultimately, with any baking you do, make sure you have fun, don't be afraid to experiment and, most importantly, trust the process.

EQUIPMENT LIST

ESSENTIALS

Baking tray
Line a baking tray (pan) with baking parchment and use it for a variety of bakes from cookies to scones to caramelised white chocolate.

Cake tins
Preferably use a loose-bottom or springform tin (pan). It comes in handy for a variety of bakes, not just cakes, and the bakes are easier to remove from the tin. You can also use a silicone mould as an alternative. The 10 cm (4 in) tin is the perfect size for bento cakes, but you could also bake the cake on a baking tray (pan) and cut it out using a cookie cutter.

Cupcake/muffin tin
Typically used for cupcakes, but it can also be used for deep dish cookies (page 70) and mini tarts (page 104). It's also great for making individual portions of things, such as cookies or brownies. It's a great basic tool with a variety of uses.

Loaf tin
This is obviously great for loaf cakes, but can also be used to make smaller traybakes such as brownies.

Rolling pin
This is required for a variety of recipes for biscuits and doughs. I've seen people use wine bottles as an alternative, but just make sure the label has been removed and the bottle is clean.

Silicone madeleine tray
I prefer to use a silicone tray as I don't just use the trays for baking, but also during the decorating process when working with chocolate (page 43). Silicone is very beginner friendly so even if you may have made an error it's easy to remove compared to a metal madeleine tray.

Kitchen scales
My personal preference when measuring are scales over any other measurement tool. I've had different experiences with cups with different brands varying in size leading to inconsistencies so scales are a foolproof way of following a recipe and reducing unsuccessful baking.

Saucepan
This also has a variety of uses but is necessary for caramels, curds and some pastries such as choux. I'd recommend using a medium-sized one so you can use it for a variety of recipe quantities.

Hand mixer/whisk
You can use a wooden spoon for the majority of mixing but having a hand mixer helps speed up the process. Having a stand mixer helps even more as you can be hands free and complete other tasks in the meantime. You can also use a manual whisk for creams and caramels.

Mixing bowl/serving bowl
Ensure it is heatproof and you can use it for a variety of things without worrying about it not being able to withstand higher temperatures. Glass is preferred, but there are great-quality plastic bowls as well.

Spatula

Great for scraping the sides of your bowls to ensure everything is incorporated and nothing is left unmixed at the bottom or sides of your bowl.

Piping bag and piping tips

These are used for decorating cakes and other desserts. The piping bags hold the buttercream or your choice of topping and the piping tips give distinctive piping styles.

Cookie cutters (circle and flower)

These are great for cutting out biscuits, cookies, scones and other pastries and cakes. They can also be used to shape cookies so they are more circular after baking.

Wire rack

This is great for cooling your bakes, as it ensures that the bakes cools down evenly. If you use a plate the bases of your bakes will remain warmer for longer.

NON-ESSENTIALS

Turntable

This makes the cake decorating process a lot easier. The cake turning allows for a smoother finish for your cakes and makes piping a lot easier as you don't have to start and stop to manually turn the cake each time.

Ice-cream scoop

This is great for portioning cookie dough and cupcake batter and can help with consistency and accuracy across your bakes.

Blow torch

This is used to torch and caramelise sugar for things such as crème brûlée. I use it for my Crème Brûlée Basque Cheesecake (page 90), but it can also be used for torching meringue.

Food processor

This helps when making desserts like scones or shortcrust pastries as you can incorporate the butter a lot quicker into the flour without getting your hands dirty. Let it do all the work or at least as much as possible.

TIPS & TRICKS

Room temperature ingredients
It's important that your ingredients are at room temperature and are at the same temperature when baking as it makes the whole process smoother. Unless the recipe calls for specific temperatures for the ingredients, such as cold butter, aim to bake with room temperature ingredients.

Eggs
All my recipes use medium-sized eggs. For egg white recipes, such as meringue or Italian Meringue Buttercream (page 18) you can separate the egg yolks from the whites, but you can also buy pasteurised egg whites if you have no use for the egg yolks. Egg yolks can be used in custards (page 29) and curds (page 28).

Lining cake tins and trays
I personally only use a good non-stick spray. I make sure there's some lining on the base just in case, but the non-stick sprays do most of the work. Depending on the cake flavour or what I'm baking I may require extra lining (e.g. something fruit based or sticky like caramel). If you don't have a non-stick spray, grease the tin (pan) with room temperature butter and dust it with flour, or lining it with baking parchment is a great alternative.

Food colourings
Natural food colourings are great in baking using fruit powders such as raspberry and blueberry and other powders such as matcha. However, some colours are tricky to make without using food colours and these work great if you want the colour without flavouring the whole dessert. I'd recommend trying products from Colour Mill and Rainbow Dust.

Infused sugars
I always like to have a variety of infused sugars in my kitchen at all times. You can create vanilla sugar from used vanilla pods, or infuse your sugar with fresh lavender or rosemary sprigs. All you need to do is fill an airtight container with caster (superfine) sugar and add one or two vanilla pods (beans) or flavouring of choice. Just remember to top up the sugar every now and then.

Mise en place
This French phrase means 'putting in place' or 'gathering'. Measure out your ingredients and components for a recipe ahead of time, as this makes the whole baking process a lot smoother. You know everything is measured correctly and most importantly you know you have all the ingredients you need before you start baking.

Shop-bought pastries
There's nothing wrong with using a little help from time to time for your pastries, tarts, etc, so the baking process doesn't feel too intimidating, but it sure does feel great when you've made everything from scratch yourself. Don't be too hard on yourself and give it a go, but know you have store-bought options as a backup.

Dummy cakes
Using polystyrene dummies is a great way to practise designs and your piping techniques without the wastage of an actual cake. As it's polystyrene underneath you can just scrape off or wash your 'cake' before trying another design. You can use a quick and easy buttercream like American Buttercream (page 20) if you don't want to waste buttercreams like Italian Meringue Buttercream (page 18).

BAKING MYTHS

You need to sift your flour

I personally don't notice a huge difference if I sift my flour or not as the main way I incorporate air into my cakes is creaming the butter and sugar. I only ever sift if I'm using ingredients such as icing (confectioners') sugar or cocoa (unsweetened chocolate) powder.

Baking margarines are bad

Stork is my preferred margarine for cakes, which I personally feel creates a softer, more moist cake. Unsalted butter can work as an alternative but if using it then I would recommend adding about 1 tablespoon yoghurt or milk for every 100 g (3.52 oz) of unsalted butter to your cake batter to help create a softer cake.

Don't need salt in baking

False! Salt a lot of the time enhances your bakes such as Salted Caramel (page 24) or chocolate cake so if a recipe includes it, use it!

Oven temperatures are always accurate

Oven temperatures aren't always the temperature you've set it to and can vary slightly. Most bakes such as cakes won't be majorly affected if the temperature is a little bit high or low by around 5–10 degrees, but depending on what you're baking if you require a specific temperature I'd invest in an oven thermometer to ensure it's the right temperature as every oven is different. Fan ovens can be stronger so lower the temperature by 5–10 degrees, but most importantly get to know your oven.

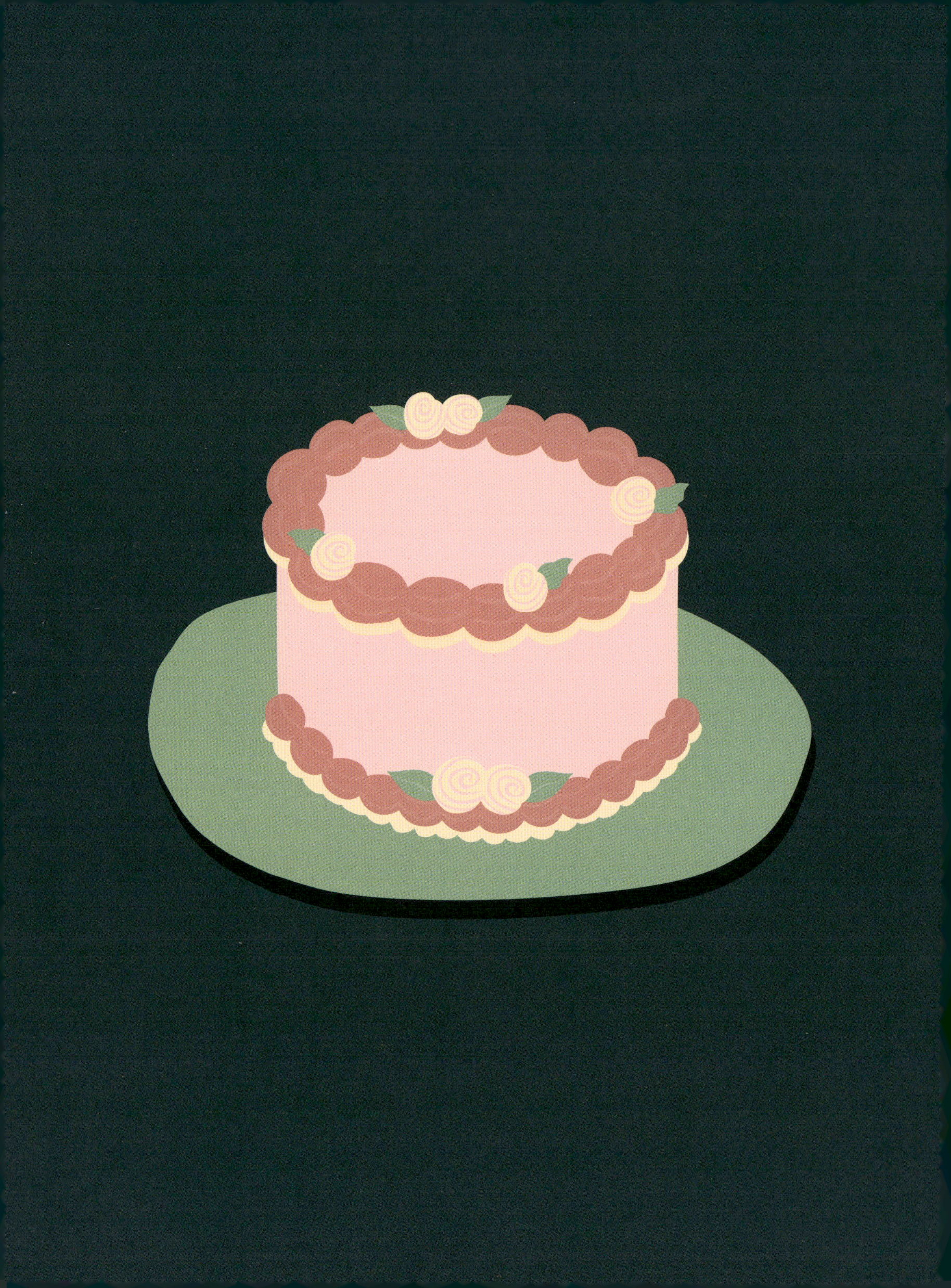

Basics

These are the fundamentals of my baking and they are recipes I've been collecting, adapting and curating over the years. These are great for you to use as bases then you can experiment and adapt them, adding your own twists to make them your own.

Italian Meringue Buttercream / 18

Cream Cheese Frosting / 20

American Buttercream / 20

Mock 'Meringue' Buttercream / 21

Ganache / 22

Caramelised White Chocolate / 23

Salted Caramel / 24

Sugar Syrup / 25

Brown Butter / 26

Strawberry Jam / 27

Lemon Curd / 28

Custard / 29

Biscuits / 30

Shortcrust Pastry / 31

Italian Meringue Buttercream

Makes enough for 1 x 15 cm (6 in) cake or 3 bento cakes

This is my go-to recipe that I've used for years and is a staple in my kitchen. Since I tried meringue-based buttercream a few years ago, I haven't looked back since. If you're not familiar with this type of buttercream give it a go.

---

100 ml (3.52 fl oz) water
300 g (10.58 oz) caster (superfine) sugar
5 large egg whites (175 g/6.17 oz)
500 g (17.6 oz) unsalted butter, at room temperature
½ teaspoon salt
1 tablespoon vanilla extract

1. Pour the water into a saucepan and add 250 g (8.81 oz) of the sugar. Place the pan on the hob and stir until the sugar dissolves. Bring the mixture to the boil while using a damp pastry brush dipped in water to clean any sugar crystals on the side of the pan. When the syrup reaches 100°C (212°F) on a sugar thermometer or starts boiling, whisk the egg whites until stiff, preferably using a stand mixer fitted with a whisk attachment. This can also be done with a heatproof bowl and a hand mixer. Gradually whisk in the remaining 50 g (1.76 oz) sugar.

2. Boil the syrup without stirring until it reaches 120°C (248°F). If you don't have a thermometer, you can check if the mixture is ready by dropping a little of the syrup into a bowl of cold water. If it's slightly sticky but still holds its shape a little it is at the hard ball stage, which is perfect. These results can vary so some trial and error may be required.

3. As soon as the syrup reaches 120°C (248°F), remove the pan from the heat to prevent the syrup from getting any hotter.

4. With your hand mixer or stand mixer on medium–high speed, gradually pour in the syrup in a thin stream on the side of the bowl so it doesn't get caught on the whisk and splatter everywhere. Continue whisking for 8–10 minutes until the bowl feels lukewarm.

5. Gradually whisk in the butter until it is fully incorporated, then add the salt and vanilla extract. Mix on low speed for 3–4 minutes with a paddle attachment if using a stand mixer or by hand if you have used a hand mixer ensure it is smooth with no air bubbles. Use straight away or store in an airtight container in the refrigerator for up to two weeks. Make sure to bring it to room temperature before using.

TIP

If your meringue is too warm it can result in a soupy buttercream, but it can be rectified. Just pop it in the refrigerator for 15 minutes, then whip it again and it will come together. Do not throw your buttercream away if it splits. It's part of the process so don't worry and keep mixing until it is smooth.

VARIATIONS

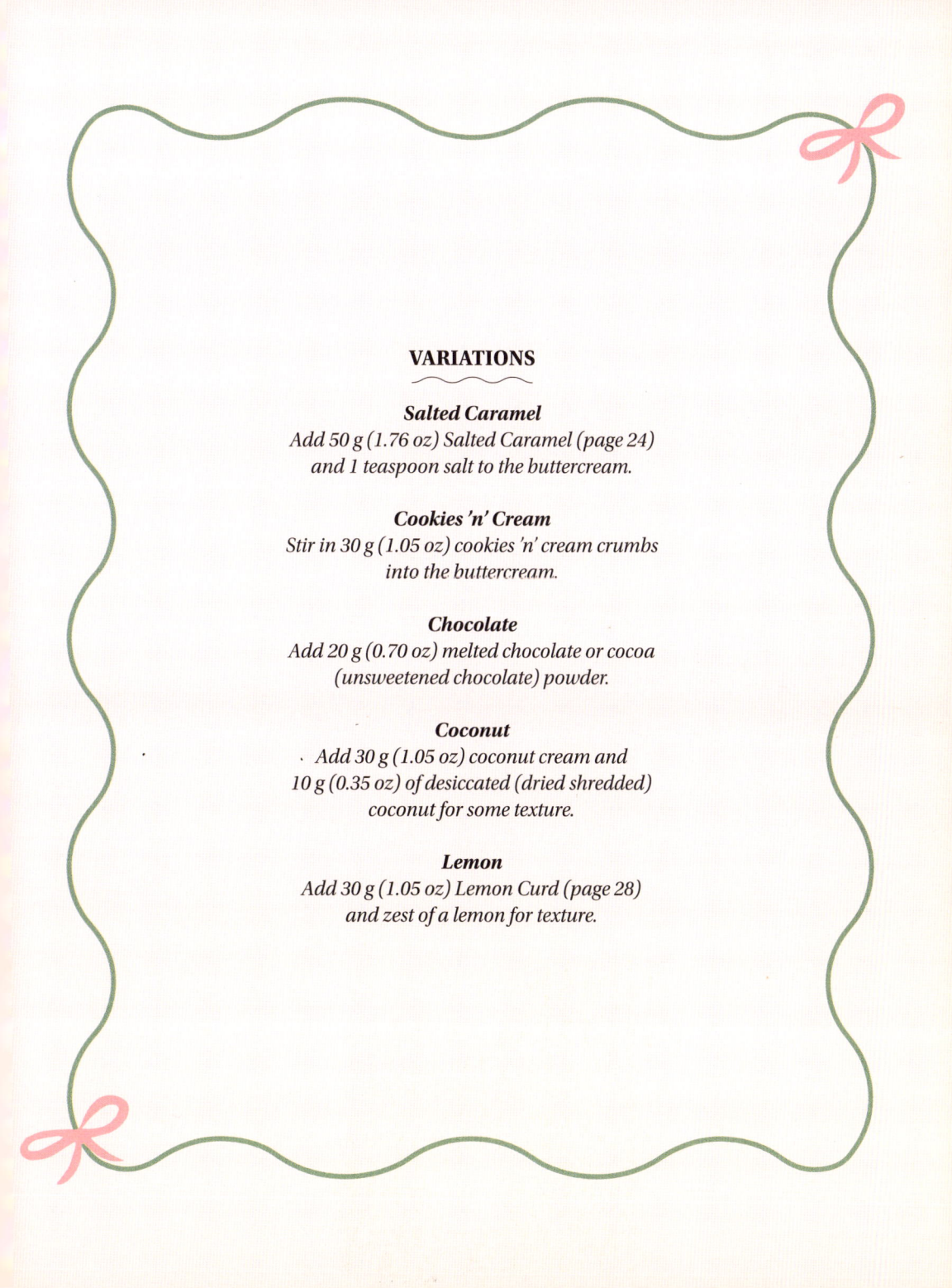

Salted Caramel
Add 50 g (1.76 oz) Salted Caramel (page 24) and 1 teaspoon salt to the buttercream.

Cookies 'n' Cream
Stir in 30 g (1.05 oz) cookies 'n' cream crumbs into the buttercream.

Chocolate
Add 20 g (0.70 oz) melted chocolate or cocoa (unsweetened chocolate) powder.

Coconut
Add 30 g (1.05 oz) coconut cream and 10 g (0.35 oz) of desiccated (dried shredded) coconut for some texture.

Lemon
Add 30 g (1.05 oz) Lemon Curd (page 28) and zest of a lemon for texture.

Cream Cheese Frosting

Makes enough to frost 1 loaf cake or fill and thinly coat 1 x 15 cm (6 in) cake

This is a great alternative to buttercream as it is thick enough to fill and coat a cake. It works a treat for a traditional red velvet cake or another dessert.

---

300 g (10.58 oz) icing (confectioners') sugar, sifted
50 g (1.76 oz) unsalted butter, at room temperature
125 g (4.4 oz) cold cream cheese

1. Beat the icing sugar and butter together until the mixture is combined. It will have a breadcrumb-like consistency. This can be done by hand with a wooden spoon, a hand mixer or a stand mixer.

2. Add the cream cheese and mix until it is fully incorporated, then continue mixing for 3–4 minutes until the frosting is light and fluffy. Use or store it in an airtight container in the refrigerator for up to a week.

American Buttercream

Makes enough for 1 x 15 cm (6 in) cake or 3 bento cakes

This is another great buttercream recipe to have in your repertoire. It is easier and quicker than a meringue-based buttercream (page 18). It's also a little sweeter but good to still try just in case you need it.

---

650 g (22.9 oz) icing (confectioners') sugar, sifted
500 g (17.6 oz) unsalted butter, at room temperature

TIP
If the buttercream is too thick, you can add some hot water/warm milk to loosen the mixture slightly.

1. Sift the sugar into a large bowl and set aside.

2. Beat the butter in a stand mixer fitted with a paddle attachment or in a bowl with a hand mixer for 5 minutes, or until it is a pale yellow colour.

3. Add the sugar to the butter in two batches and beat for 5 minutes. Use immediately or store in an airtight container in the refrigerator for up to two weeks. Make sure you bring it to room temperature before using.

BASICS

Mock 'Meringue' Buttercream

Makes enough to frost and thinly coat 1 x 15 cm (6 in) cake

This is a great egg-free alternative to traditional buttercream. It's silky like meringue buttercream but has a slightly sweet taste like American Buttercream (page 20).

---

150 g (5.29 oz) whole milk, at room temperature
300 g (10.58 oz) icing (confectioners') sugar, sifted
375 g (13.22 oz) unsalted butter, at room temperature
1 tablespoon vanilla extract

1. Using a hand mixer, combine the milk and sugar in a large bowl until fully incorporated. You can also use a stand mixer.

2. Add the butter and whisk on low speed for 2 minutes. Add the vanilla and increase the speed to medium–high. Continue whisking until fluffy. The mixture will go through a curdled stage, but it will eventually come together. Use immediately or store in an airtight container in the refrigerator for up to two weeks. Make sure you bring it to room temperature before using.

BASICS

Ganache

Example for 15 cm (6 in) two-layer cake

Ganache is a great coating option, but depending on your ratio of chocolate to cream it can be quite versatile. Here is a small guide to ganache ratios and what you can use them for.

---

double (heavy) cream
chocolate of your choice, chips or chopped chocolate

DARK AND MILK CHOCOLATE – 2:1 RATIO
200 g (7.05 oz) double (heavy) cream
400g (14.10 oz) dark or milk chocolate

WHITE CHOCOLATE – 3:1 RATIO
200 g (7.05 oz) double (heavy) cream
600 g (21.16 oz) white chocolate

Microwave Method

Add the cream and chocolate to a heatproof bowl and microwave on 30-second bursts until the cream is heated. Leave to stand for 1 minute, then stir until it is smooth. Use as needed.

Hob Method

Add the chocolate to a heatproof bowl and set aside. Heat the cream in a small saucepan until just boiling. Once the cream is hot pour over the chocolate and allow to stand for about 1 minute before stirring until smooth.

TIPS

If the chocolate splits it may be because you have overheated the ganache, but using a dash of cold double cream will bring the ganache back to life.

CHOCOLATE TO CREAM RATIOS:

DARK AND MILK CHOCOLATE
1:1 ratio: glazes and fillings
2:1 ratio: thicker ganache, perfect for truffles
1:2 ratio: thin pourable ganache for dipping

WHITE CHOCOLATE
3:1 ratio: firmer ganache for coating and covering cakes
2:1 ratio: great for drips

Caramelised White Chocolate

Makes about 150 g (5.29 oz)

This is essentially liquid gold. Well, not quite but once you've tried it you will want to find lots of different recipes to use it in. You can adjust the quantity of white chocolate to your liking as the method is the same regardless of the amount.

---

200 g (7.05 oz) white chocolate chips

1. Preheat the oven to 160°C fan (350°F) and spread the chocolate chips on the tray.

2. There's need to line as the heat from the pan helps the chocolate melt more efficiently. Bake for about 20 minutes, taking the tray out every 4–5 minutes to give the chocolate a good stir and smooth out any lumps. It may become chalk-like and get very crumbly at times, but just keep stirring until it smooths out.

3. Once the chocolate has caramelised and darkened in colour, remove from the oven and leave to cool on the tray to room temperature, then transfer to the refrigerator to set. Once set, break it up into chunks and it's ready to use. Store in an airtight container in the refrigerator for up to a month.

Salted Caramel

Makes about 150 g (5.29 oz) caramel

This is another staple in my kitchen that works well on its own as a sauce, a filling for a cake or incorporated into a buttercream or ganache. Make sure you use a large saucepan as the mixture will expand once the cream is added.

---

30 g (1.05 oz) water
100 g (3.52 oz) granulated sugar
75 g (2.64 oz) double (heavy) cream
25 g (0.88 oz) cold unsalted butter, cut into cubes
1 tablespoon salt, or to taste

1. Add the water and sugar to a large saucepan and stir to combine, then heat over a medium heat until the sugar has dissolved.

2. Increase the heat to high and bring to the boil. Don't stir after this and let the mixture continue boiling for 5 minutes, or until it turns an amber colour. Keep an eye on it constantly as it can change very quickly.

3. Remove the pan from the heat and slowly whisk in the cream. The mixture will bubble up quite a bit, so be careful. Stir in all the butter and leave to cool slightly before adding the salt.

4. Pour the caramel sauce into a bowl and leave to cool completely. Store in an airtight container in the refrigerator for up to two weeks. The caramel will thicken up more once it's cooled and refrigerated.

Sugar Syrup

Makes enough syrup for 3–4 bento cakes or 1 x 15 cm (6 in) cake

A sugar syrup helps to bring more moisture to your cakes, and it can also help infuse flavour into the cakes like lemon juice or a liqueur. This recipe can be increased or decreased as needed – just use equal parts sugar and water.

100 g (3.52 oz) caster (superfine) sugar
100 g (3.38 oz) water

1. Combine the sugar and water in a saucepan and heat for 2 minutes, or until the sugar has melted. Cool completely, which should take about 10 minutes, then transfer to an airtight container. Alternatively, you can heat the sugar and water in the microwave in a heatproof bowl for 2 minutes until the sugar has dissolved. Store in an airtight container in the refrigerator for up to two weeks.

Brown Butter

Makes 75 g (2.64 oz)

This small change to butter makes a big difference and can really intensify the flavour of your cookie, cake or buttercream. It's always good to have some on stand by in your refrigerator.

---

100 g (3.52 oz) unsalted butter

1. Add the butter to a saucepan and melt over a medium heat, stirring constantly. Once melted, the butter will begin to foam. Keep stirring and after 5–6 minutes the butter will turn golden brown. The milk solids will turn brown at the bottom of the pan and the butter will have a very nutty scent. It's now ready to use or you can transfer to a heatproof bowl and cover with cling film (plastic wrap) or to an airtight container and, once it has cooled down, store in the refrigerator for up to two weeks.

Strawberry Jam

Makes about 200 g (7.05 oz) jam

This is a great recipe for a filling for a variety of desserts. You can also replace strawberries with another fruit, although I'd recommend a berry-type fruit such as blueberries or raspberries. The main thing is to keep the fruit and sugar the same amount.

---

300 g (10.58 oz) strawberries, fresh or frozen
300 g (10.58 oz) granulated sugar

1. Add the strawberries and sugar to a large saucepan. Bring to the boil, stirring.

2. Reduce the heat slightly and simmer for 30 minutes, stirring occasionally, or until the mixture coats the back of a spoon to the point where you can draw a line through it with your spoon and it holds its shape.

3. Transfer the mixture to a heatproof bowl, then cover the surface of the jam with cling film (plastic wrap). Make sure the cling film is touching the jam to prevent it forming a skin. Alternatively you can use a clean sterilised jar (see tip below). Chill in the refrigerator for at least 2 hours, or until you need it. It will thicken as it sets, then use at your desired consistency. Store in the refrigerator for up to a week.

TIPS

For a thicker jam, add 1 teaspoon of pectin.

To sterilise a jar, place the jar in a large saucepan or pot, cover it with water and boil for 10–15 minutes. Using tongs, remove from the pan and allow to air-dry.

BASICS 27

Lemon Curd

Makes about 200 g (7.05 oz) curd

This is another versatile recipe where you can replace the lemons with fruit such as limes or mangoes.

---

zest of 1 lemon
50 g (1.76 oz) lemon juice
100 g (3.52 oz) caster (superfine) sugar
60 g (2.02 oz) butter
2 eggs, beaten

1. Add the lemon zest, juice, sugar and butter to a heatproof bowl set over a pan of simmering water. Stir occasionally until the butter has melted. Then, using a small whisk or fork, stir in the beaten eggs. Keep gently whisking the mixture over the heat for 10 minutes, or until thickened. Keep stirring so you don't cook the egg and end up with scrambled egg pieces.

2. Pour the cooked curd through a sieve (fine mesh strainer) into a sterilised jar (page 27) or clean bowl and cover. Once it has cooled, store in the refrigerator for up to 2 weeks.

TIP

To thicken the curd, add 1 teaspoon of cornflour (cornstarch) when adding the lemon juice.

Custard

Makes about 300 g (10.58 oz)

Personally I find the process of making your own custard very satisfying and rarely buy store-bought custard anymore. Try this recipe and see for yourself.

---

260 g (9.17 oz) whole milk
2 egg yolks
25 g (0.88 oz) cornflour (cornstarch)
65 g (2.29 oz) caster (superfine) sugar
30 g (1.05 oz) cold unsalted butter, cut into cubes

1. Heat the milk in a large saucepan to a low simmer, just before it comes to a boil.

2. Meanwhile, mix the egg yolks, cornflour and sugar together in a heatproof bowl. Set aside.

3. Once the milk is hot, pour a small amount, about 3 tablespoons, into the egg and sugar mixture and whisk together. Don't add all the milk at once or you could cook the eggs and end up with scrambled egg pieces in your custard.

4. While whisking, slowly pour the rest of the milk into the egg and sugar mixture until it is fully combined. Pour the mixture back into the saucepan and heat over a medium-low heat, stirring constantly, until the mixture thickens and coats the back of your spoon to the point where you can draw a line through it with your spoon and it holds its shape.

5. Stir in all the cold butter at once until melted, then pour the custard into a heatproof bowl. Cover the surface of the custard with cling film (plastic wrap), making sure the cling film touches the surface to prevent a skin forming. Once it has cooled, store in the refrigerator until required. It will keep for three days.

TIPS

For a more caramelised flavour, replace the sugar with light brown sugar.

Once the custard is cooked, strain it through a sieve (fine mesh strainer) into the bowl to make sure there are no pieces of egg and it's completely smooth.

Biscuits

Makes 15–20 biscuits
(depending on size)

This dough doesn't need to be chilled and can be rolled and cut out to bake straight away as there is minimal spreading during cooking. Have fun with cookie cutters to create different shapes.

---

400 g (14.10 oz) plain (all-purpose) flour
50 g (1.76 oz) granulated sugar
50 g (1.76 oz) caster (superfine) sugar
1 teaspoon baking powder
1 teaspoon salt
125 g (4.40 oz) unsalted butter, at room temperature
125 g (4.40 oz) golden syrup
1 egg

1. Line a large baking sheet with baking parchment.

2. Add all the dry ingredients and the butter to a large bowl and mix together with your fingertips until the butter is fully incorporated and the mixture resembles breadcrumbs. You can also use a stand mixer.

3. Mix the golden syrup and egg together in a small bowl, then mix into the dry ingredients until fully combined and the bowl is relatively clean. You can either wrap the dough in cling film (plastic wrap) and refrigerate until needed, or roll and cut it out to your desired thickness and shape.

4. If baking the biscuits right away, preheat the oven to 170°C fan (375°F) and place them on the prepared baking sheet. Bake for 15–18 minutes until golden brown. If you'd like a biscuit with a bit more of a snap, bake for an extra 2 minutes. If not using straight away or you have extra dough, wrap in cling film and keep it in the refrigerator for up to a week.

TIP

For gingerbread biscuits, replace 40 g (1.41 oz) of the granulated sugar with light brown sugar and add 2 tablespoons of ground ginger, 1 tablespoon of ground cinnamon and 1 teaspoon of ground nutmeg.

Shortcrust Pastry

Makes enough for 1 galette or 6–8 mini tarts

This is a quick and easy pastry recipe that can be used across a variety of desserts, from tarts to galettes. The key is to keep the pastry as cold as possible.

- 175 g (6.17 oz) plain (all-purpose) flour
- 100 g (3.52 oz) cold unsalted butter, cut into cubes
- 25 g (0.88 oz) icing (confectioners') sugar
- 1 egg yolk
- 1 tablespoon cold water

1. Add the flour, butter and sugar to a food processor and pulse a few times until it is a breadcrumb-like consistency.

2. Add the egg yolk and water and pulse again until the mixture forms into a ball. Tip the dough onto a sheet of cling film (plastic wrap), wrap up and refrigerate for 30 minutes, or until needed. The dough lasts for up to a week.

TIP
If you don't have a food processor, don't cut your butter but use a grater to make the butter easier to incorporate.

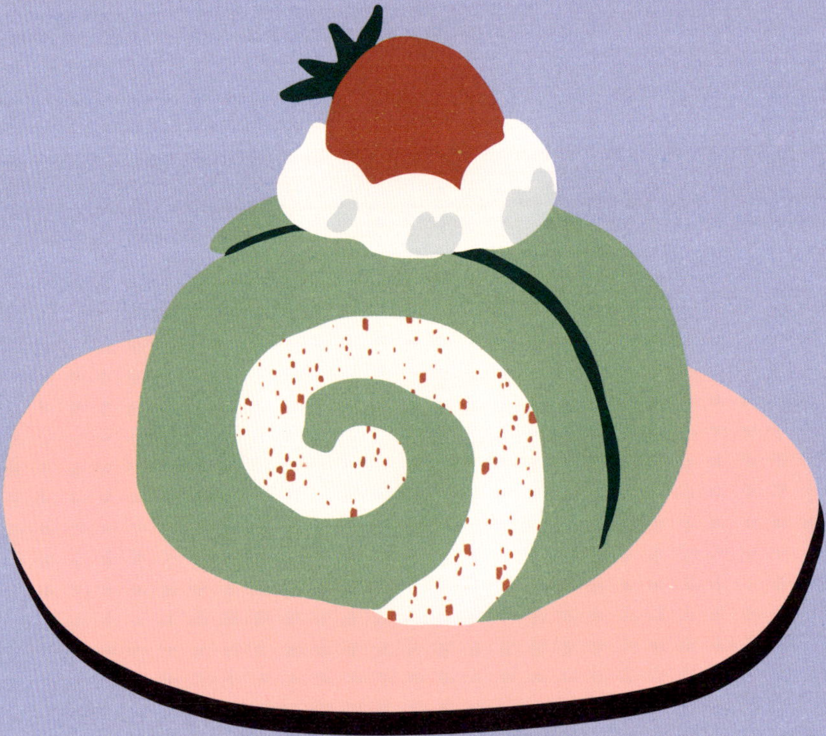

Cakes

Cakes are likely to be the first thing someone makes when they bake for the first time, but cakes come in so many different forms. This chapter contains some of my most signature recipes and techniques, which are great to start with, as well as recipes I have used over the years with some new and fun flavour combinations for you to try.

Vanilla Cake / 36

Vanilla Madeleines / 42

Chocolate-covered Cherry Madeleines / 46

Chocolate-covered Edible
Flower Madeleines / 47

Raspberry & Orange Blossom Friand / 48

Apple Cinnamon Crumb Cake / 50

Matcha & Strawberry Swiss Roll Cake / 52

Chocolate Cake with Brown Butter
Cream Cheese Frosting / 54

Salted Caramel Banana Bread / 57

Raspberry Eton Mess Mini Cakes / 58

Olive Oil & Orange Loaf Cake / 60

BENTO CAKES

Vanilla Cake

Makes 3 bento cakes or
1 x 15 cm (6 in) cake layer

This is my base for pretty much all my cakes. It's also the first recipe I learnt when I first started baking at a young age with my mum. It's super simple and a great recipe to have in your repertoire.

non-stick spray or unsalted butter, for greasing
150 g (5.29 oz) unsalted butter or baking spread
150 g (5.29 oz) caster (superfine) sugar
3 eggs
150 g (5.29 oz) self-raising flour
¼ teaspoon salt
1 teaspoon vanilla bean paste

1. Preheat the oven to 170°C fan (375°F). Grease three 10–15 cm (4–6 in) cake tins (pans) or silicone moulds.

2. Using a hand mixer, mix the butter and sugar together for 2 minutes until fluffy. Alternatively, mix in a bowl with a wooden spoon.

3. Add the eggs, one at a time, and mix until they are incorporated. Add the flour and salt and mix until fully combined. Scrape down the sides and bottom of the bowl with a spatula to ensure everything is mixed together properly, then add the vanilla and mix until combined.

4. Divide the batter evenly between the prepared tins, about 200 g (7.05 oz) per tin, and level with a spatula. Bake for 20–22 minutes until golden brown and a skewer inserted into the centre of each cake comes out clean. Leave in the tins or moulds for 2 minutes, then tip out onto a wire rack to cool completely.

TIP
If you are short on time, you can do the all-in-one method by mixing all the ingredients at once until they are fully combined.

VARIATIONS

Chocolate
Omit 20 g (0.70 oz) of the self-raising flour and add 30 g (1.05 oz) cocoa (unsweetened chocolate) powder.

Salted Caramel
Replace 50 g (1.76 oz) caster (superfine) sugar with light brown sugar and add an extra ½ teaspoon of salt. Sandwich the cakes with Salted Caramel (page 24).

Lemon
Add zest of a lemon and make a Sugar Syrup (page 25) with the juice of the lemon, then spoon over the sponge straight out of the oven.

Red Velvet
Omit 10 g (0.35 oz) of the self-raising flour and add 20 g (0.70 oz) cocoa (unsweetened chocolate) powder and a few drops of red food colouring until your desired shade of red. Sandwich the cakes with Cream Cheese Frosting (page 20).

White Chocolate and Raspberry
Add 30 g (1.05 oz) frozen raspberries to the batter and sandwich the cakes with white chocolate Ganache (page 22) and buttercream of your choice (pages 18–21).

Cookies 'n' cream
Add 40 g (1.41 oz) cookie pieces or crumbs and sandwich the cakes with a cookies 'n' cream buttercream (page 19).

Coconut and Lime
Add 20 g (0.70 oz) desiccated (dried shredded) coconut and the zest of a lime. Sandwich the cakes with lime curd (page 28) and decorate with Coconut Buttercream (page 19).

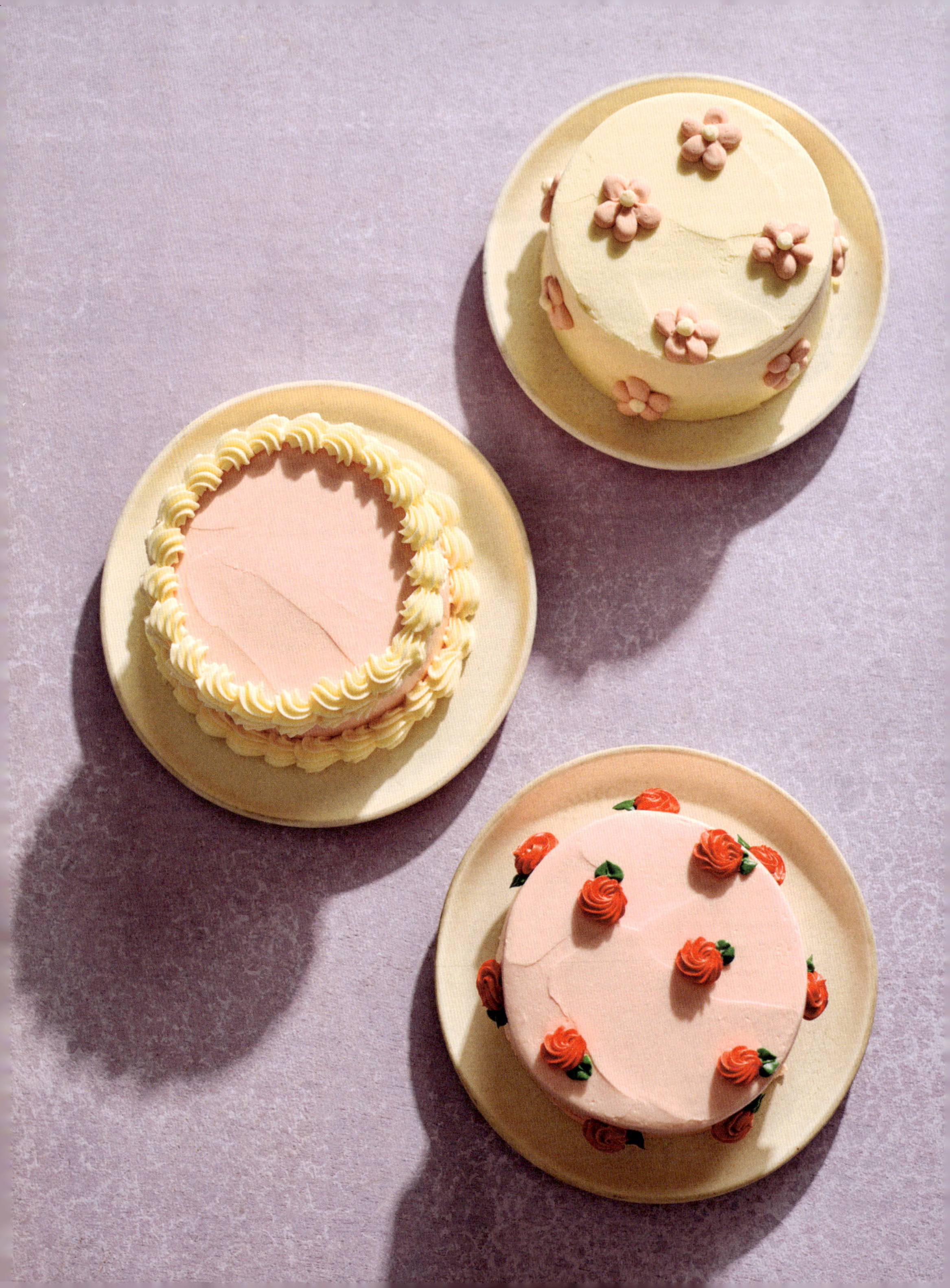

CAKE TIPS

Crumb coat

Crumb coating your cakes is when you have stacked and filled your cakes then covered the sponge in buttercream. This locks in the crumbs of the cake so that when you add your final coat of buttercream it will have a nice, crumb-free finish.

Buttercream dam for softer/runnier fillings

Think of a buttercream dam as a border for your cakes. Piping a ring of buttercream around the edges of your cake layer acts as a barrier for your fillings, which may be a little soft or runny like a curd or caramel. This helps to prevent any leakages when stacking your cakes.

Couplers

These are small inserts for piping bags that allow you to change the piping tip without having to use another piping bag. It is very efficient if you're using the same colour for multiple details on a cake and saves on the number of piping bags used.

BUTTERCREAM PIPING TECHNIQUES/STYLES

STAR

Shell
When looked at from the side this piping technique looks like seashells. Squeeze the piping bag with even pressure, pull your piping bag up slightly to give it a bit of height then bring the bag back down and drag the buttercream slightly to define the shell shape. For the next shell go back over the end of the previous shell and repeat to continue the shell pattern and make it look like a shell chain.

Rosette
Start in the centre then gradually pipe a circle, making the circle slightly wider as you complete the loop. If you pipe the circle on the same spot you'll give the swirl height rather than having it flat.

ROUND

Heart
You're going to make a slightly wide V shape so start from the left-hand side and pipe a straight diagonal line about 2.5 cm (1 in) long, applying a bit more pressure at the start so the line has a slight round bubble start and thins out towards the end. From the right-hand side, pipe another diagonal line about 2.5 cm (1 in) long, meeting it at the bottom of the first line and make a heart shape.

Flower
Pipe five small round bubbles in a circle pattern meeting in the middle until you have completed your circle and have a flower. Apply a bit more pressure at the start so the petals have a slight round bubble tip and thin out towards the end. You can pipe a small dot in the same or different colour to bring your flower to life.

PETAL

Ruffles
Start with the smaller part of the piping tip outward then move the piping tip in and out or up and down for your desired pattern. This works great for the border of a cake.

Curved ruffles
Similar to the ruffles for borders, move the piping tip up and down slightly while creating a curved arch shape around the sides of your cake until you complete the sides. You can also do straight ones by dragging the tip from point to point without creating ruffles.

LEAF

Leaves
Ensure the piping tip is on the side and not flat so the pointed tip is facing upwards, then apply even pressure and create small leaves. These are great for adding leaves onto piped flowers or rosettes to make them look flower-like and realistic.

Ruffles
Similar to the leaves but instead of a single leaf keep applying pressure and drag the piping bag while squeezing, then go back on yourself and continue piping in the same way as the shell technique. This works well for the border of your cake.

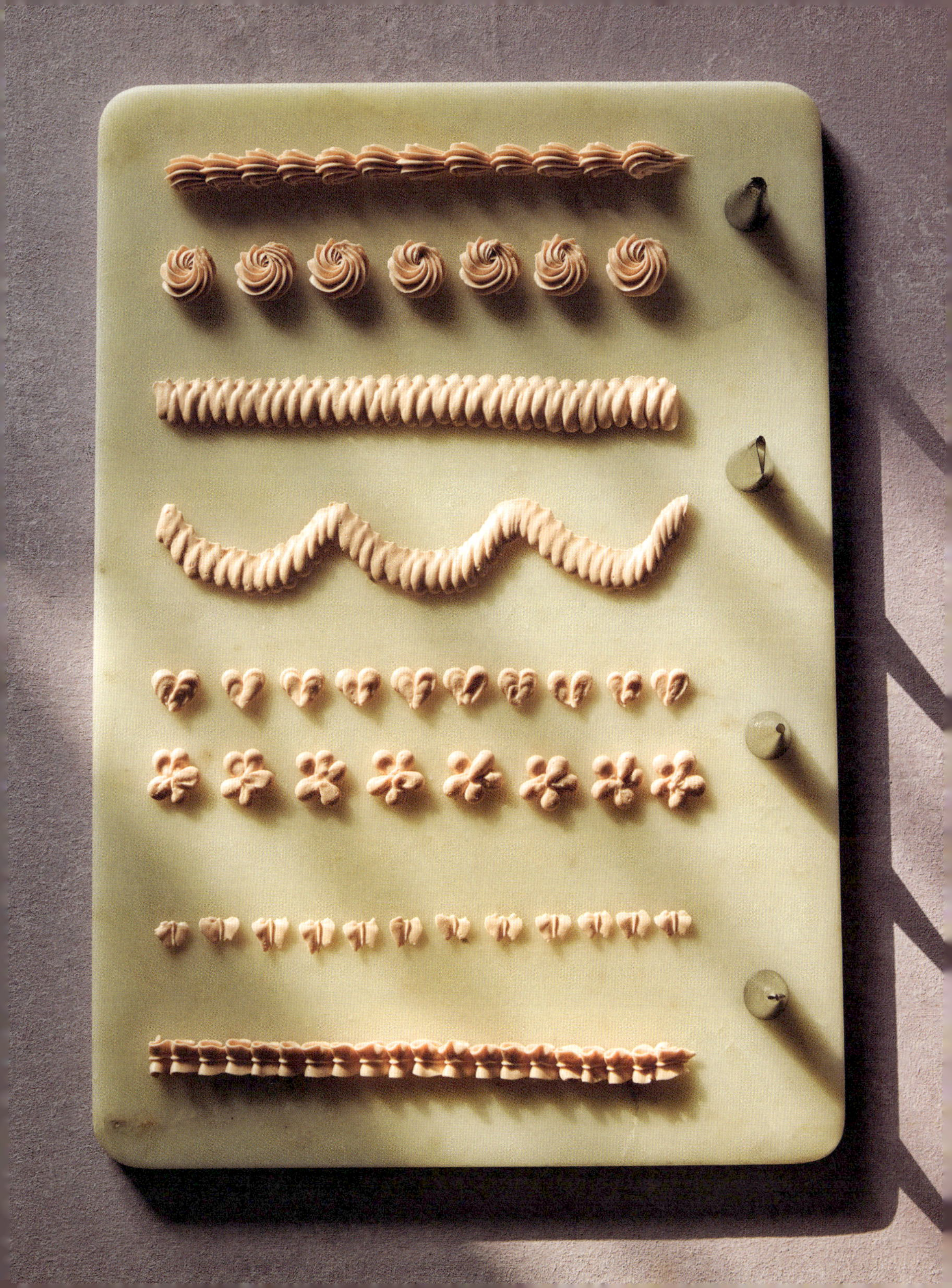

MADELEINES

Vanilla Madeleines

Makes 8–9 madeleines

Madeleines are another staple in my kitchen and are the base of one of my most popular products: my chocolate-covered madeleines (pages 46 and 47). Traditionally, you'd use a metal madeleine tray but I use a silicone mould as I usually cover them with chocolate. If you're just baking plain madeleines, then a metal tray will be absolutely fine.

---

non-stick spray or melted unsalted butter, for greasing
1 egg
50 g (1.76 oz) caster (superfine) sugar
65 g (2.29 oz) plain (all-purpose) flour
½ teaspoon baking powder
1 tablespoon vanilla bean paste
50 g (1.76 oz) unsalted butter, melted and cooled
2 tablespoons icing (confectioners') sugar, for dusting

1. Spray a silicone madeleine mould with a oil or brush with melted butter.

2. Whisk the egg and caster sugar together in a large bowl until frothy. Lightly whisk in the flour, baking powder and vanilla.

3. Fold in the cooled melted butter, then leave the batter to stand in the refrigerator for 30 minutes or more.

4. Preheat the oven to 170°C (375°F). Transfer the batter to a piping bag and pipe the batter into the prepared mould, or use a spoon. Bake for 12–14 minutes until golden brown.

5. Transfer the madeleines to a wire rack and leave for a few minutes to cool, then dust with icing sugar and enjoy. Store them in an airtight container for up to five days.

VARIATIONS

Chocolate
Add 2 tablespoons cocoa (unsweetened chocolate) powder to the batter.

Earl Grey
Add 2 tablespoons of ground Earl Grey to the batter. Brush the baked madeleines with an icing glaze using 100 g (3.52 oz) icing (confectioners') sugar, 1 tablespoon water and a little ground Earl Grey, then allow to set.

Lemon and Elderflower
Add the zest of a lemon to the batter. Brush the baked madeleines with an elderflower glaze using 100 g (3.52 oz) icing sugar and 1 tablespoon elderflower cordial, then allow to set.

Blood Orange
Add the zest of a blood orange to the batter. Brush the baked madeleines with a blood orange glaze using 100 g (3.52 oz) icing sugar and 1 tablespoon blood orange juice, then allow to set.

TIP

The batter can be prepared the night before. The colder the batter the better as the shock of cold batter and a hot oven helps with the signature madeleine bump.

MELTING CHOCOLATE

Melting chocolate can be a little tricky at first but after a couple of times you will get used to the process. If you are melting chocolate regularly I recommend investing in a sugar or infrared thermometer.

Add white chocolate to a heatproof bowl and melt in the microwave in short bursts of 20–30 seconds, stirring after each increment so it doesn't overheat and burn. Melt until there are still a couple of unmelted pieces of chocolate then use the residual heat to melt the unmelted pieces. If you have a thermometer the chocolate should be about 28–29°C (82.4–84.2°F) before using. If you don't have a thermometer, dip a small piece of baking parchment into the chocolate and leave it to stand on the work surface at room temperature for 2 minutes. If it goes slightly shiny and has a smooth surface it's ready to use.

TIPS

If the chocolate is too warm you can add pieces of unmelted chocolate and stir until you bring the temperature down.

If you are using milk chocolate you are looking for the temperature to be about 29–30°C (84.2–86°F) before using. If you are using dark chocolate you're looking for the temperature to be around 31–32°C (87.8–89.6°F) before using.

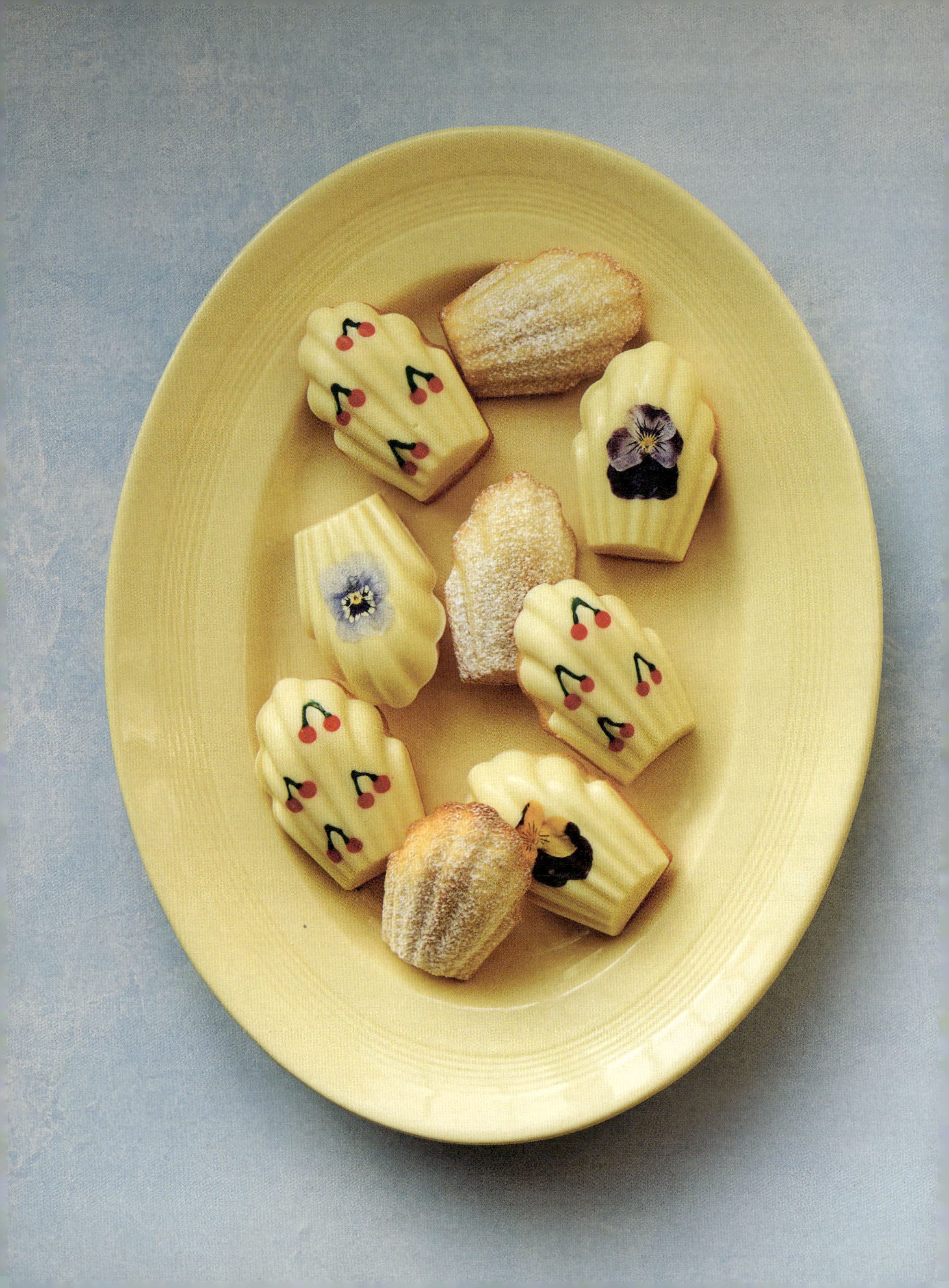

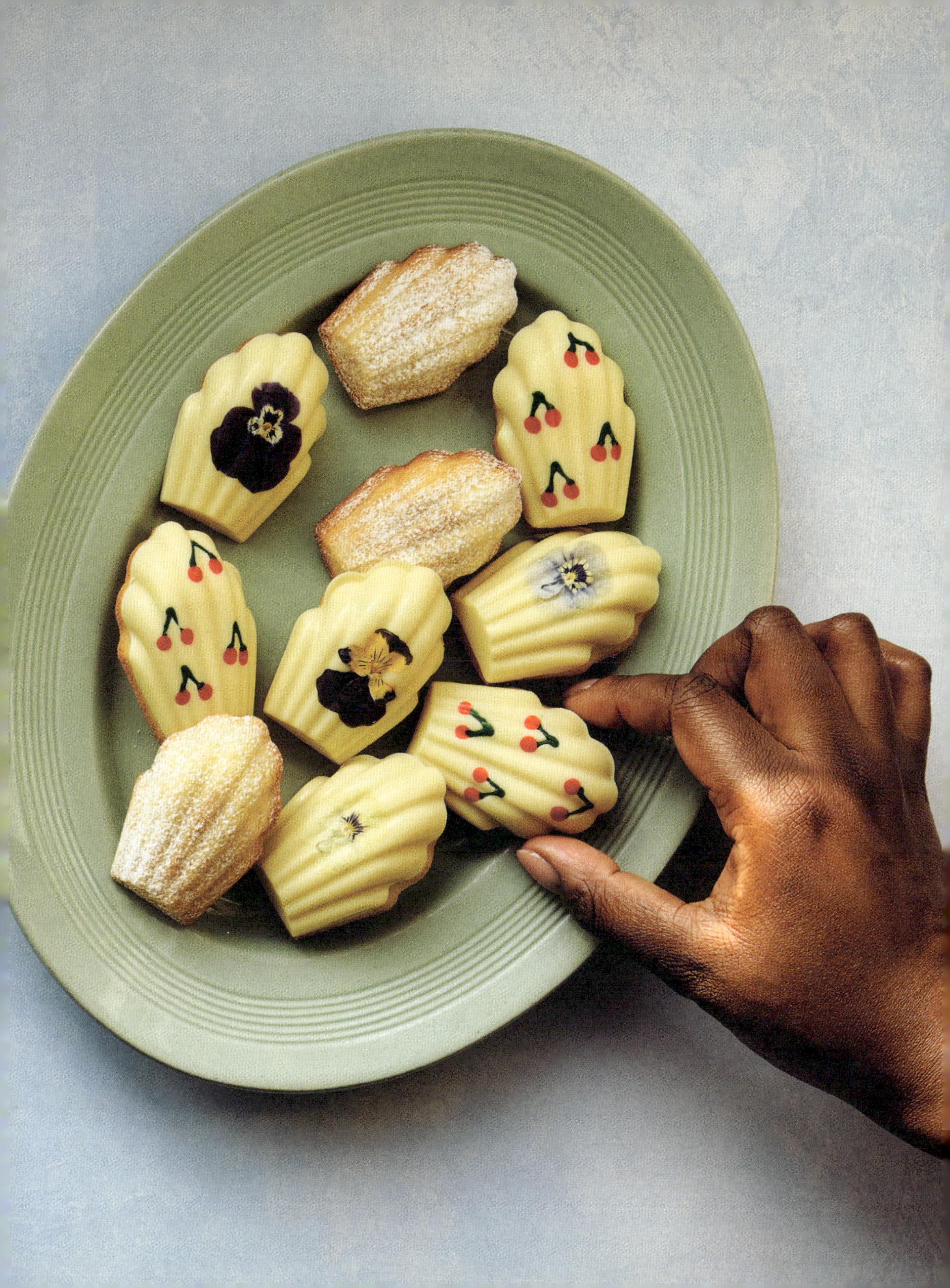

Chocolate-covered Cherry Madeleines

Makes 8–9 madeleines

These were one of the first designs I ever did and they have become a staple at Dee's Basement. They are very simple to create but look extremely attractive and make a statement. They are a really cool twist on a classic madeleine.

---

1 batch of Vanilla Madeleines, baked and cooled (page 42)
200 g (7.05 oz) white chocolate, melted (page 43)
red food colouring
green food colouring

1. Make a batch of madeleines according to the instructions on page 42.

2. Colour 20 g (0.70 oz) of the melted white chocolate red and another 20 g (0.70 oz) of the melted white chocolate green and spoon into separate piping bags. Set the remaining white chocolate aside.

3. In each cavity of a clean and ungreased silicone mould, pipe two red dots followed by a green upside-down V shape to join the two dots on the ends so it resembles a bunch of cherries. You can do one large cherry in the middle or smaller cherries dotted around the cavity. Leave to set in the refrigerator for 30 minutes or until hard.

4. Cover the piped cherry design and no more than half of each cavity with the remaining melting white chocolate.

5. Push a baked and cooled madeleine into the mould and chocolate until the chocolate is visible around all the edges, then repeat with the remaining madeleines until all the cavities are filled. Leave to harden in the refrigerator for 30 minutes.

6. Once chilled and hardened, remove the madeleines from the mould and enjoy!

TIP
Make sure you use oil-based food colouring as water-based food colouring won't mix properly with the chocolate.

Chocolate-covered Edible Flower Madeleines

Makes 8–9 madeleines

I wanted a floral twist decoration on some madeleines, so I incorporated some edible flowers. These come in so many varieties, allowing you to create designs with different styles and colours. Violas are my go-to flowers as the colours are so versatile, but you can also use pansies, rose petals or primula flowers.

---

1 batch of Vanilla Madeleines, baked and cooled (page 42)
dried edible flowers
200 g (7.05 oz) white chocolate, melted (page 43)

1. Make a batch of madeleines according to the instructions on page 42.

2. Place an edible flower into each cavity of a clean and ungreased silicone mould, with the back of the flower facing you so the front of the flower is on the front of the madeleine, then spoon in the melted chocolate on top.

3. Press the madeleines into the mould and leave to set in the refrigerator for 30 minutes, or until hard.

4. Remove the madeleines from the mould and enjoy.

TIP
Try to use dried edible flowers as they are preserved and thinner compared to fresh edible ones, which won't last as long and have more texture.

CAKES

Raspberry & Orange Blossom Friand

Serves 6

These mini almond cakes are simple to make and flavoursome, especially when paired with raspberries and orange blossom.

---

non-stick spray or unsalted butter, for greasing
120 g (4.23 oz) unsalted butter
120 g (4.23 oz) icing (confectioners') sugar, sifted
50 g (1.76 oz) ground almonds
50 g (1.76 oz) plain (all-purpose) flour
3 egg whites (100 g/3.52 oz)
50 g (1.76 oz) raspberries
10 g (0.35 oz slivered almonds (optional), to decorate

For the glaze

10 g (0.35 oz) raspberries, plus extra to decorate
100 g (3.52 oz) icing (confectioners') sugar
1 teaspoon orange blossom water

1. Preheat the oven to 170°C fan (375°F) and grease 6 holes of a cupcake tin (pan) or whichever mould you'll be using with butter or non-stick spray. Melt the butter in a saucepan or microwave, then leave to cool.

2. Mix the sugar, ground almonds and flour together in a large bowl.

3. Add the egg whites to another bowl and whisk lightly with a fork until frothy.

4. Pour the egg whites into the flour mixture with the melted butter and mix well.

5. Pour the mixture into the prepared tin and add a few raspberries to each one. Bake for 20–25 minutes until the friands are risen and springy and a skewer inserted into the centre comes out clean. Remove the friands from the tin and allow to cool completely on a wire rack.

6. Meanwhile, make a glaze by crushing the raspberries in a bowl with a fork. Add the icing sugar and orange blossom water and mix until combined. Spoon the glaze over the friands and decorate with extra raspberries and almond slivers (if using). They are best eaten the same day but can be stored in an airtight container in the refrigerator for up to two days.

TIP

You can use frozen raspberries to reduce wasting a full pack of fresh raspberries, if you like.

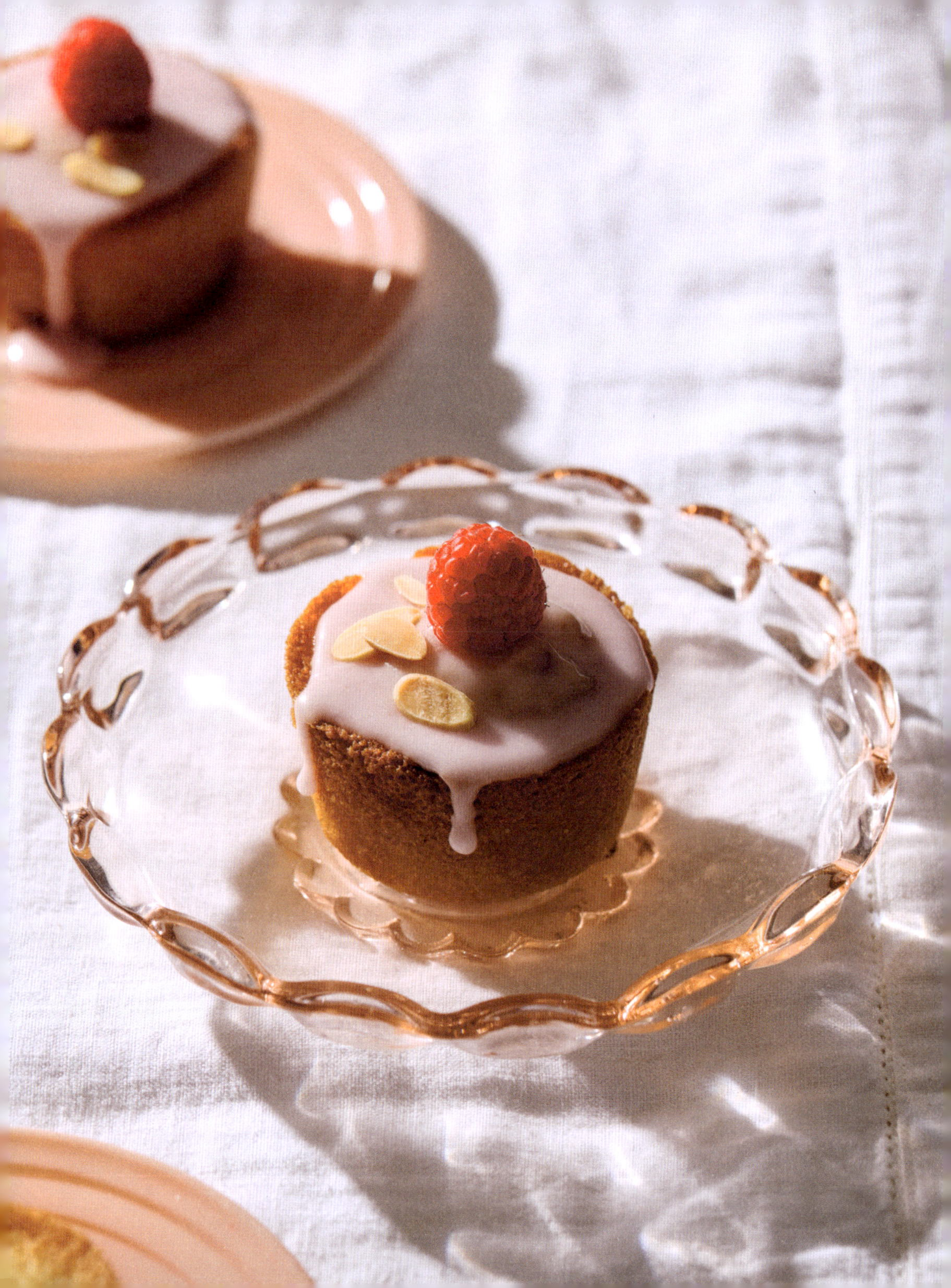

Apple Cinnamon Crumb Cake

Serves 6

This recipe combines both cake and crumble for a delicious treat that's perfect to eat on its own or with some Custard (page 29).

---

non-stick spray or unsalted butter, for greasing
100 g (3.52 oz) unsalted butter or baking spread
100 g (3.52 oz) caster (superfine) sugar
100 g (3.52 oz) self-raising flour
2 eggs
1 tablespoon vanilla bean paste
1 apple, peeled, cored and chopped
1 tablespoon ground cinnamon, for tossing
icing (confectioners') sugar, for dusting (optional)

For the crumble topping

50 g (1.76 oz) packed light or dark brown sugar
25 g (0.88 oz) granulated sugar
1 tablespoon ground cinnamon
½ teaspoon salt
50 g (1.76 oz) unsalted butter, melted
100 g (3.52 oz) plain (all-purpose) flour

1. Preheat the oven to 170°C fan (375°F). Grease and line a 15 cm (6 in) cake tin (pan) with baking parchment.

2. For the crumble topping, mix both sugars, the cinnamon and salt together in a medium bowl. Stir in the melted butter, then gently mix in the flour with a fork. Don't overmix and keep the mixture as large crumbles. If overmixed, it will turn into a thick paste. Set aside.

3. Add the butter, caster sugar, flour, eggs and vanilla to a large bowl and mix until they are well incorporated. Pour the cake batter into the prepared tin.

4. Toss the chopped apple in the cinnamon, then arrange on top of the cake batter. Sprinkle over the crumble mixture.

5. Bake for 25–30 minutes until a clean skewer inserted into the centre of the cake comes out clean. Remove from the oven and allow to cool before removing from the tin. Once cooled, sprinkle the cake with a dusting of icing sugar (if using) and serve. Store in an airtight container for up to five days.

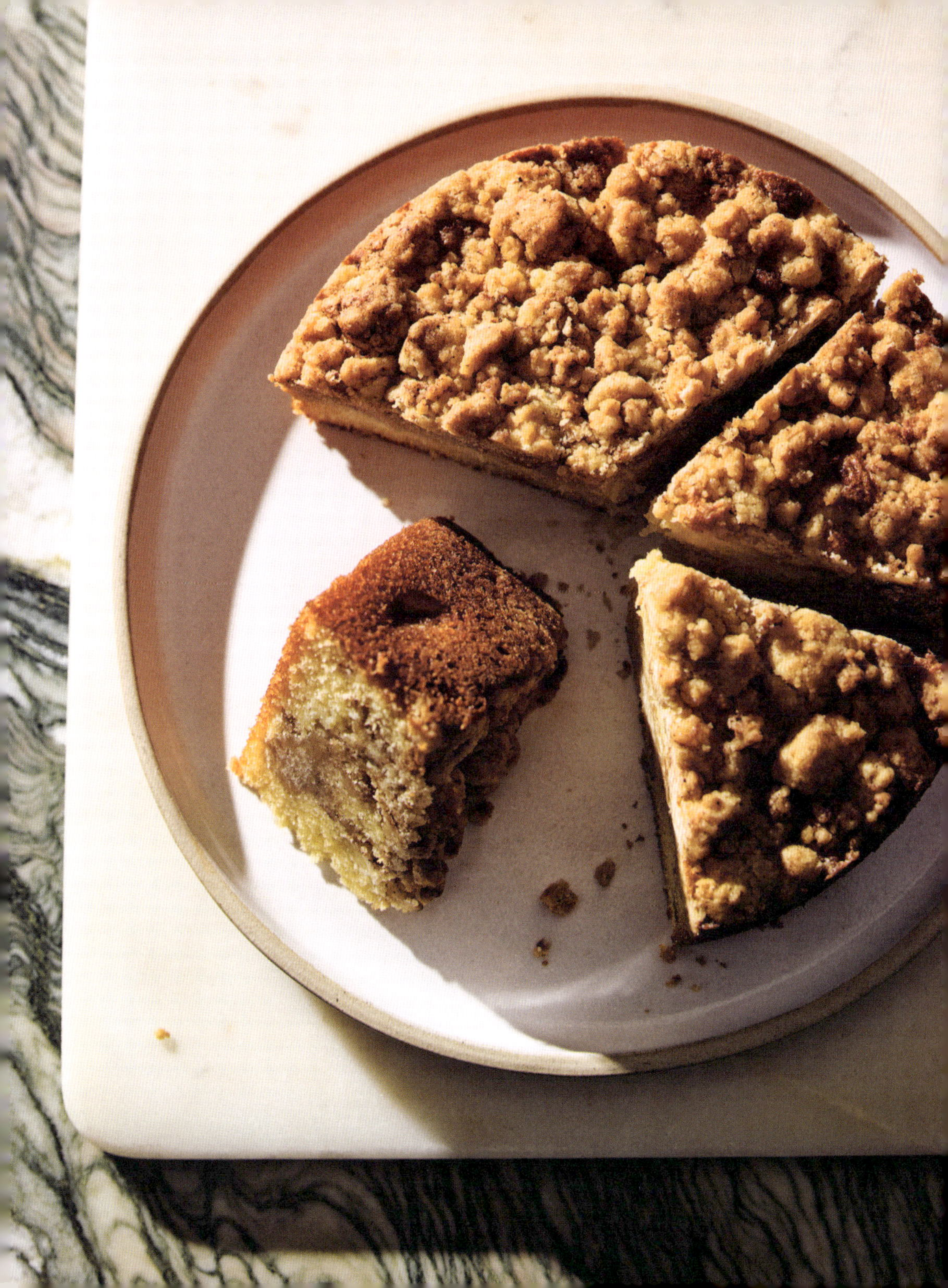

Matcha & Strawberry Swiss Roll Cake

Serves 6

The flavour combination of matcha and strawberry goes really well in this cake. The matcha also gives the cake a natural cool shade of green.

---

4 eggs, separated
80 g (2.82 oz) granulated sugar
40 g (1.41 oz) whole milk
40 g (1.41 oz) flavourless oil, such as vegetable oil
1 teaspoon vanilla extract
30 g (1.05 oz) plain (all-purpose) flour
30 g (1.05 oz) cornflour (cornstarch)
2 tablespoons matcha powder
1 teaspoon cream of tartar
icing (confectioners') sugar, for dusting

For the filling

100 g (3.52 oz) double (heavy) cream
20 g (0.70 oz) icing (confectioners') sugar
100 g (3.52 oz) Strawberry Jam (page 27)

To decorate

whipped cream, leftover from the filling
3 strawberries, halved

TIP

If you overwhip the cream and it curdles, mix in some more double (heavy) cream until you get your desired consistency.

1. Preheat the oven to 170°C fan (375°F) and line a shallow baking tray, about 25 x 38 cm (10 x 15 in), with baking parchment.

2. In a large bowl, beat the egg yolks and 20 g (0.70 oz) of the granulated sugar together for 2 minutes, or until the mixture is a pale yellow colour.

3. Mix the milk, oil and vanilla together in another bowl, then add this to the egg yolk mixture. Add the flour, cornflour and matcha powder to the bowl and stir to combine.

4. In a separate bowl, whisk the egg whites, cream of tartar and the remaining granulated sugar together until stiff peaks form. Fold the whisked egg whites into the matcha batter until everything is fully combined.

5. Pour the batter into the prepared tray and smooth with a spatula, making sure the batter reaches all the corners of the tray. Bake for 15–16 minutes until springy to the touch.

6. Set a sheet of baking parchment on top of a clean tea (dish) towel and with icing sugar. Run a thin knife around the edge of the cake and flip it onto the baking parchment. Peel off the baking parchment on the bottom of the cake and place a fresh sheet of baking parchment on top. Starting on the short side, carefully roll up the cake tightly and set aside until ready to fill.

7. To make the filling, using a hand whisk, whip the cream and icing sugar together in a medium bowl until creamy and spreadable. Carefully unroll the cake, then spread with the raspberry jam followed by the whipped cream. Roll the cake back up, transfer it to a plate and cut into slices. Finish off with a swirl of whipped cream and a strawberry half.

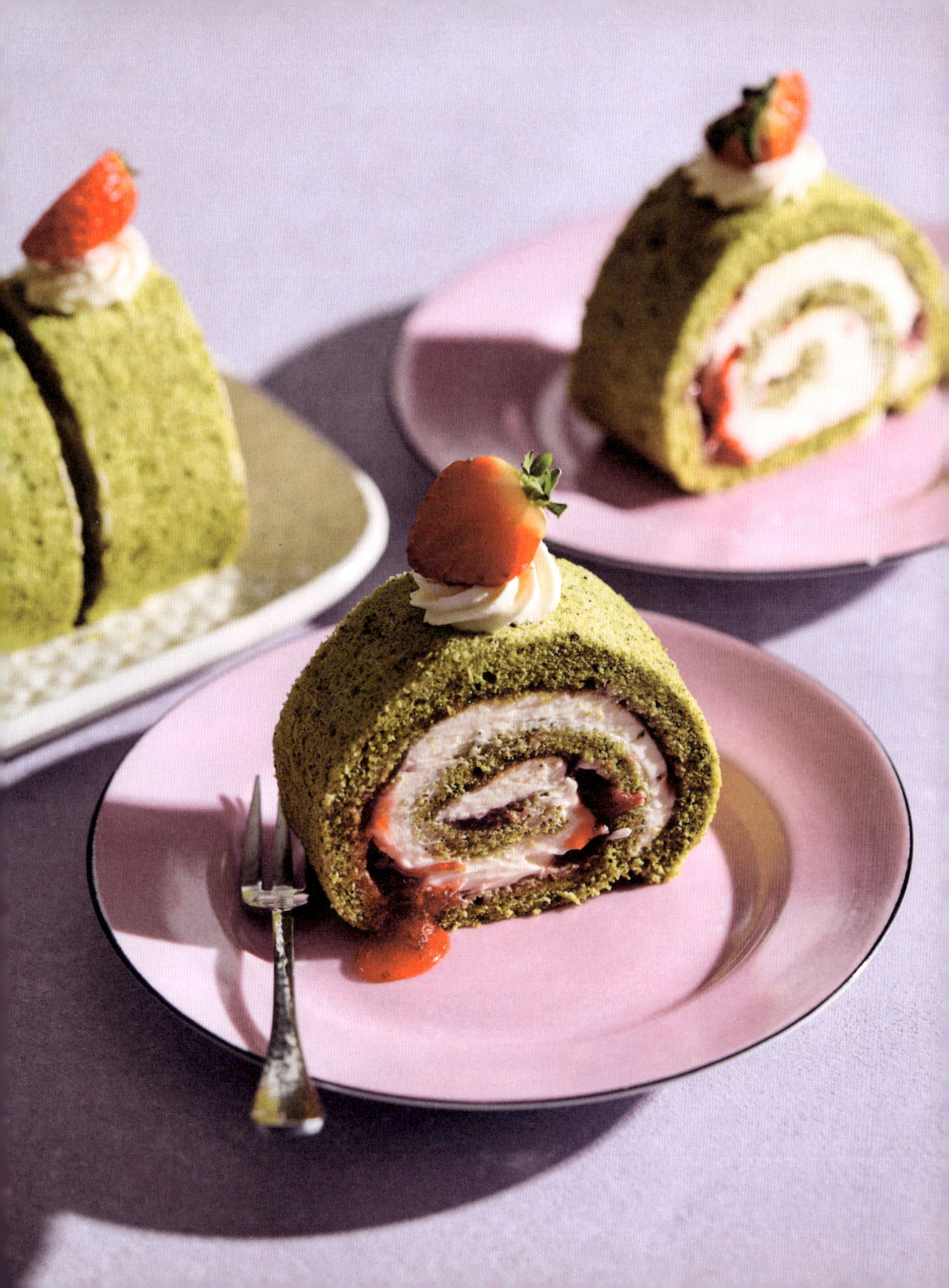

Chocolate Cake *with* Brown Butter Cream Cheese Frosting

Serves 5–6

This is a very fudgy, decadent chocolate cake that contrasts well with the cream cheese frosting. You will definitely eat more than one slice of this cake!

---

non-stick spray or unsalted butter, for greasing
105 g (3.70 oz) plain (all-purpose) flour
150 g (5.29 oz) granulated sugar
40 g (1.41 oz) cocoa (unsweetened chocolate) powder, sifted
¾ teaspoon bicarbonate of soda (baking soda)
¼ teaspoon baking powder
½ teaspoon salt
1 egg
85 ml (2.87 fl oz) buttermilk
30 g (1.05 oz) vegetable or flavourless oil
85 ml (2.87 fl oz) hot water
1 batch of Cream Cheese Frosting (page 20)
10 g (0.35 oz) Brown Butter, at room temperature (page 26)

1. Preheat the oven to 170°C fan (375°F) and grease and line a 450 g (1 lb) loaf tin (pan) with baking parchment.

2. Mix the flour, sugar, cocoa powder, bicarbonate of soda, baking powder and salt together in a large bowl and set aside.

3. In a separate bowl, whisk the egg, buttermilk and oil together.

4. Add the wet mixture to the dry ingredients, then, while stirring, gradually add the hot water until everything is just combined and the batter is smooth. Don't overmix.

5. Pour the batter into the prepared loaf tin and bake for 30 minutes, or until a clean skewer inserted into the centre of the cake comes out clean.

6. Once baked, leave the cake in the tin for 5 minutes, then remove and allow to cool completely on a wire rack.

7. Make the cream cheese frosting according to the instructions on page 20, adding the brown butter to it. Spread the frosting over the top of the cake and serve. Best eaten immediately, but it keeps for up to two days.

TIPS

If you would like a signature split down the middle of your loaf when it's baked, then pipe some room temperature butter down the middle of the loaf before baking.

You can make your own buttermilk by using 1 teaspoon lemon juice or white wine vinegar to 80 ml (2.82 fl oz) milk. Leave to stand for 2 minutes before using.

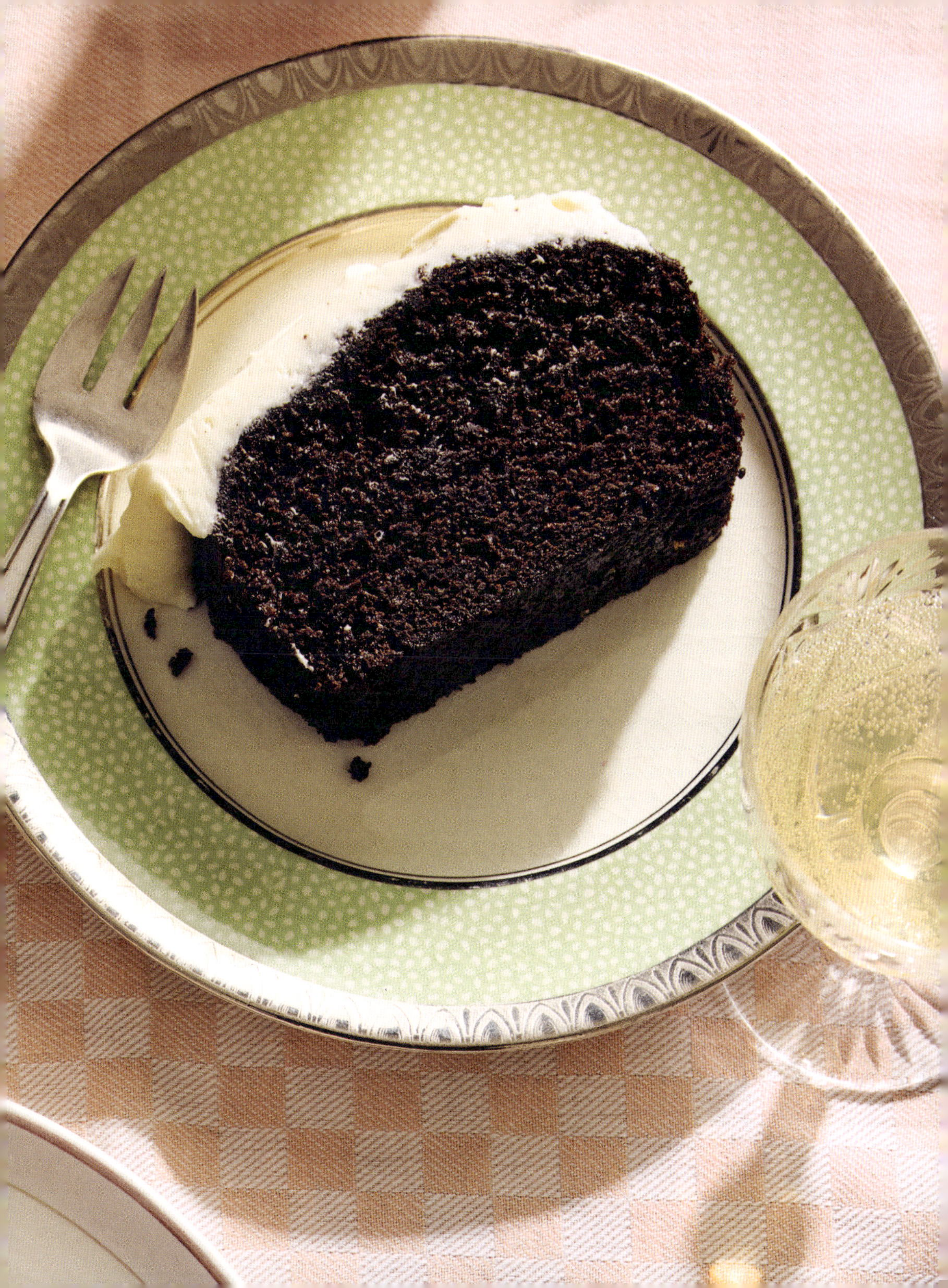

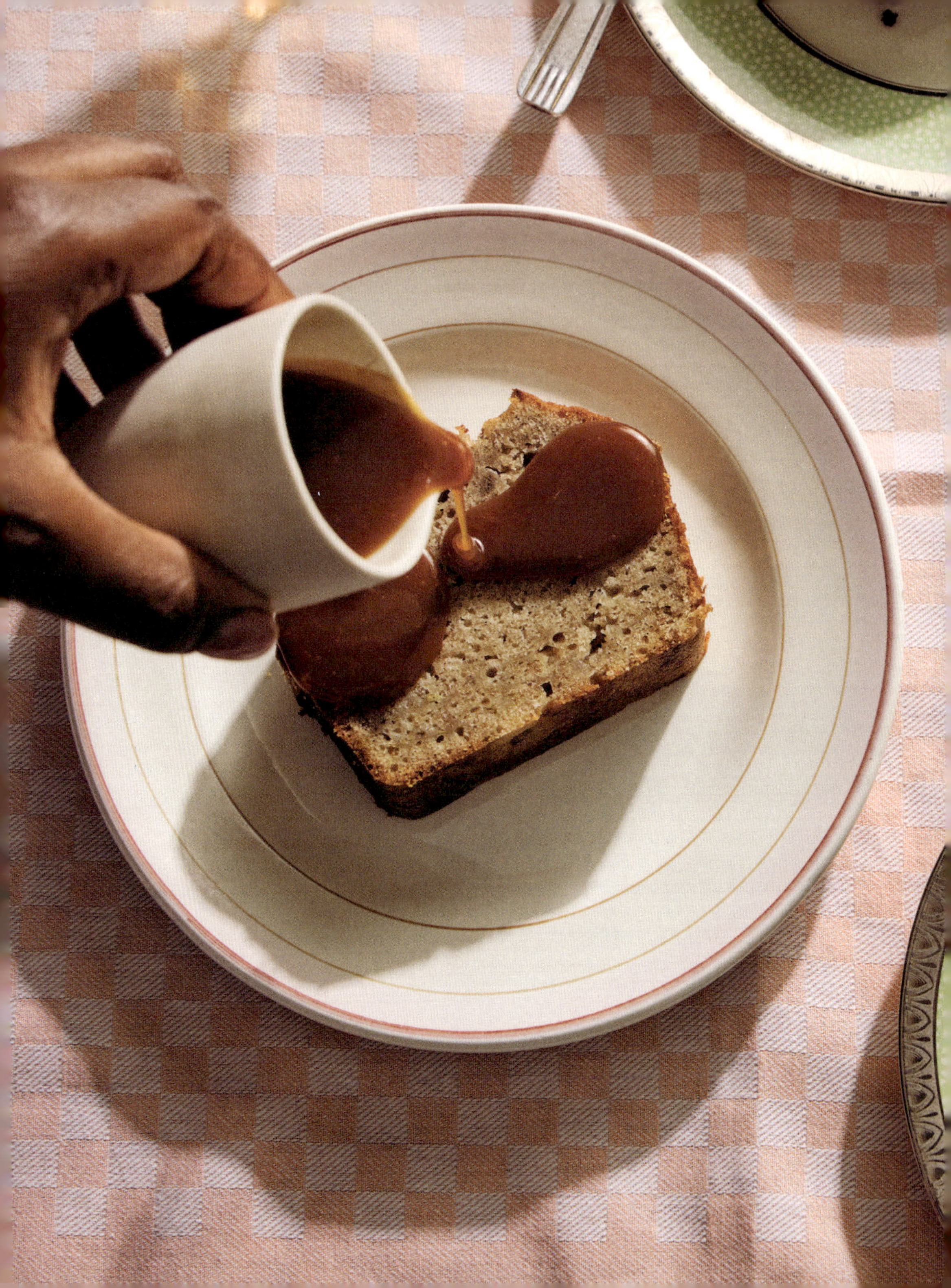

Salted Caramel Banana Bread

Serves 5–6

This is one of my favourite recipes that I use on a regular basis. It's a great way to use any overripe bananas you don't want to go to waste.

---

non-stick spray or unsalted butter, for greasing
225 g (7.93 oz) plain (all-purpose) flour
1 teaspoon baking powder
1 teaspoon ground cinnamon
½ teaspoon salt
3 ripe bananas
60 g (2.02 oz) vegetable oil
60 g (2.02 oz) unsalted butter,
10 g (0.53 oz Brown Butter (page 26)
160 g (5.64 oz) caster (superfine) sugar
2 eggs
1 batch of Salted Caramel (page 24), to serve

1. Preheat the oven to 170°C fan (375°F) and grease and line a 450 g (1 lb) loaf tin (pan) with baking parchment.

2. Whisk the flour, baking powder, cinnamon and salt together in a large bowl and set aside.

3. In another bowl, mash the bananas with the oil using a fork and set aside.

4. Whisk the butters and sugar together in a separate bowl with a hand whisk or wooden spoon until just combined, then gradually add the eggs and whisk until they are incorporated. Add the banana and oil mixture, then add the flour mixture and mix until just combined.

5. Pour the batter into the prepared loaf tin and bake for 25–30 minutes until golden brown and a skewer inserted into the centre of the cake comes out clean.

6. Remove the cake from the oven, tip it out onto a wire rack and allow to cool slightly before serving with salted caramel. If not eating straight away, store in an airtight container for up to three days.

TIP

To take your banana bread to the next level, add 50 g (1.76 oz) chopped dark chocolate or chips.

Raspberry Eton Mess Mini Cakes

Makes 1 x 10 cm (4 in) cake

Eton Mess is a classic and one of my favourite desserts so incorporating those classic flavours into mini cake form is a winner.

For the cake

non-stick spray or salted butter, for greasing
100 g (3.52 oz) unsalted butter or baking spread
100 g (3.52 oz) caster (superfine) sugar
2 eggs
100 g (3.52 oz) self-raising flour
1½ teaspoons salt
1 teaspoon vanilla paste

For the meringue

2 egg whites (70 g/2.46 oz)
110 g (3.88 oz) caster (superfine) sugar
½ teaspoon cornflour (cornstarch), sifted

To assemble

100 g (3.52 oz) double cream
20 g (0.70 oz) icing (confectioners') sugar
50 g (1.76 oz) raspberry jam (page 27)
20 g (0.70 oz) fresh raspberries
mint leaves and edible flowers, to decorate (optional)

1. To make the meringue, preheat the oven to 110°C fan (275°F) and line a baking tray (pan) with baking parchment. Whisk the egg whites in an electric mixer for 3–4 minutes until just before stiff peaks form. Alternatively, use a bowl and a hand whisk. While whisking, add the caster sugar, a tablespoon at a time, until thick, glossy and the sugar has dissolved. Fold the sifted cornflour into the meringue. Spread the meringue across the prepared baking tray and bake for 20 minutes. Reduce the oven temperature to 90°C fan (200°F) and cook for a further 20 minutes, or until the meringue is crisp and dry. Remove from the oven and set aside.

2. For the cake, preheat the oven to 165°C fan (350°F) and grease two 10 cm (4 in) tins (pans) or silicone moulds.

3. Mix the butter and caster sugar together in a bowl with a hand mixer until fluffy. Alternatively, mix with a wooden spoon. Add the eggs, one at a time, and mix until incorporated. Mix in the flour and salt until they are fully combined. Scrape down the sides and bottom of the bowl with a spatula to make sure all the ingredients are mixed properly, then stir in the vanilla. Divide the batter evenly between the prepared tins or moulds (about 200 g/7.05 oz per tin), smoothing out with a spatula, then bake for 20–22 minutes until golden brown. Allow to cool for 2 minutes, then tip out onto a wire rack and leave to cool completely. Once cool, cut off the domed top so each layer is flat.

4. Using a hand whisk, whip the cream and icing sugar together in a medium bowl, then assemble and decorate your cake. Place one layer of cake on a serving plate, spread over the cream and jam, then place the other layer on top. Finish off with more cream, meringue pieces, fresh raspberries, as well as mint leaves and edible flowers (if using), and serve. Best eaten immediately but it keeps in the refrigerator for up to three days.

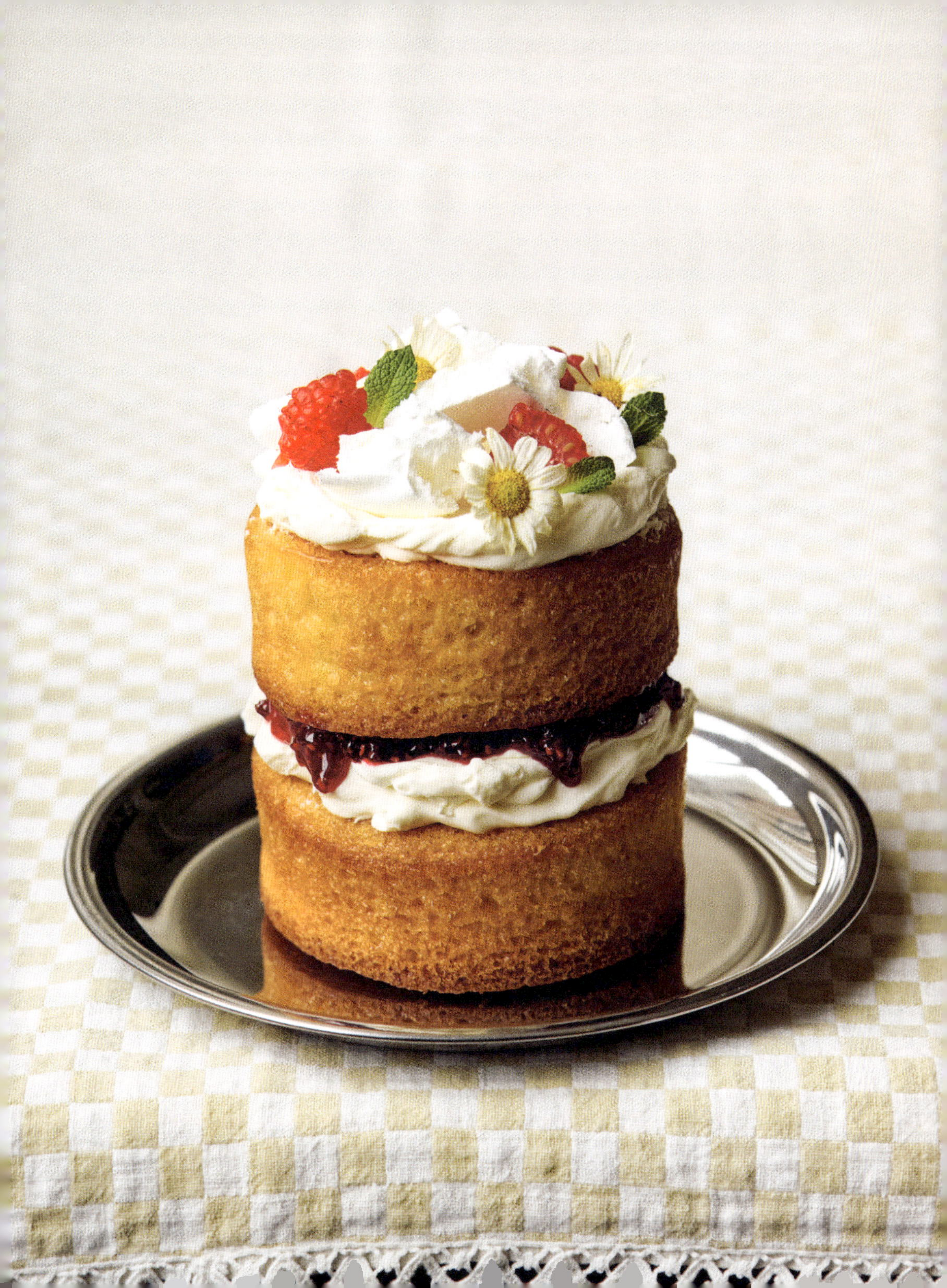

Olive Oil & Orange Loaf Cake

Makes 1 loaf cake

This is a great combination for a cake that by itself isn't too sweet so you get an extra sweetness from the sugar crumb coating.

---

non-stick spray or unsalted butter, for greasing
130 g (4.58 oz) unsalted butter, at room temperature
20 g (0.70 oz) olive oil
120 g (4.23 oz) caster sugar
3 eggs
150 g (5.29 oz) self-raising flour
20 g (0.70 oz) ground almonds
¼ teaspoon salt
zest and juice of 1 orange
10 g (0.35 oz) granulated sugar

To serve

100 g (3.52 oz) double (heavy) cream
20 g (0.70 oz) icing (confectioners') sugar
splash of olive oil (optional)

1 Preheat the oven to 170°C fan (375°F) and grease and line a 450 g (1 lb) loaf tin (pan) with baking parchment.

2 In a bowl, mix the butter, olive oil, caster sugar and orange zest until combined. Add the eggs followed by the flour, ground almonds, orange juice and salt and mix until combined. Transfer the batter to the prepared loaf tin and bake for 30–35 minutes until golden brown and a skewer inserted into the centre of the cake comes out clean.

3 Allow the cake to cool slightly before removing from the tin and leaving to cool completely on a wire rack. Once cool, sprinkle the cake with the granulated sugar.

4 Using a hand whisk, whip the cream and icing sugar together in a medium bowl, then serve a dollop with the cake, along with an extra splash of olive oil if you like.

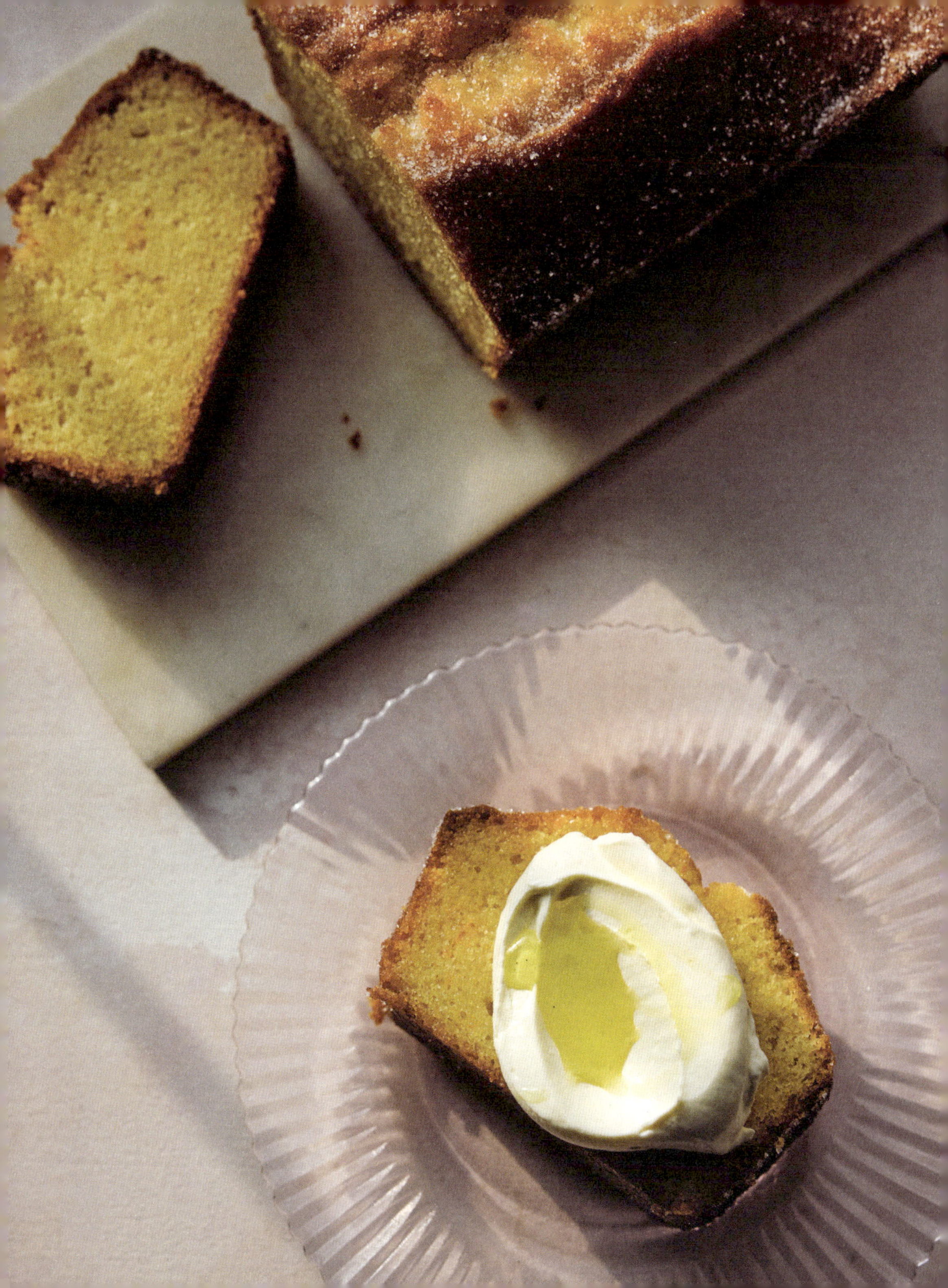

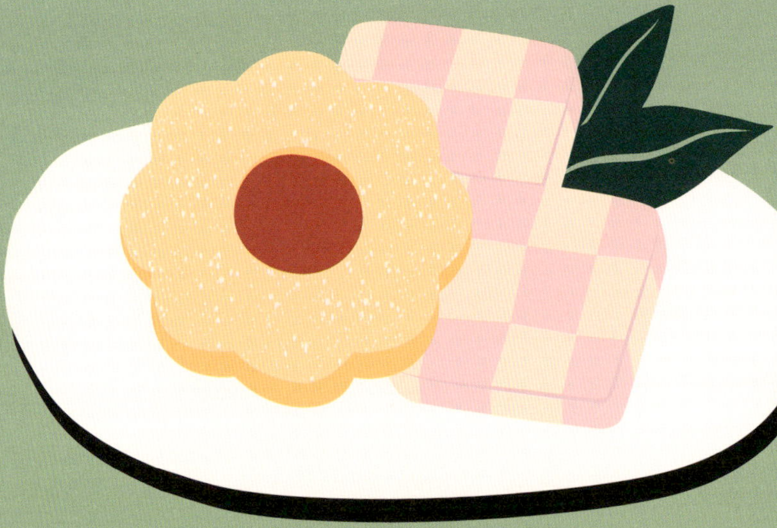

Cookies & Biscuits

From crunchy snappy biscuits to chewy cookies, these recipes will fill your kitchen with warm and delicious aromas. They are relatively straightforward to make but pack a lot of impact from the flavours and designs. These are great for baking for yourself and are also perfect to make for sweet edible gifts for family and friends.

Strawberry & Bay Leaf
Jam Biscuit Sandwich / 66

Raspberry Checkerboard Biscuits / 68

Brown Butter Pumpkin Spice
Deep Dish Cookies / 70

Lemon & Blueberry Crumble Cookies / 71

Chocolate & Caramelised White
Chocolate Cookies / 74

Brownie S'mores Cookies / 75

Lavender Shortbread / 76

Strawberry & Bay Leaf Jam Biscuit Sandwich

Makes about 8 biscuits

These are my take on a Jammie Dodger with a little twist of bay leaves in the jam.

---

300 g (10.58 oz) Strawberry Jam (page 27)
2 bay leaves
½ batch of American Buttercream (page 20)
1 batch of Biscuit dough (page 30)
plain (all-purpose) flour, for dusting
20 g (0.70 oz) icing (confectioners') sugar, for dusting

1. Preheat the oven to 170°C fan (375°F) and line a baking tray (pan) with baking parchment.

2. Make your raspberry jam according to the instructions on page 27, adding the bay leaves with the other ingredients and removing them once the jam is ready.

3. Make the American Buttercream according to the instructions on page 20 and set aside.

4. Roll out the biscuit dough on a lightly floured work surface to a thickness of 2.5 cm (1 in). Cut out 16 floral-shaped biscuits, about 7.5 cm (3 in) in diameter. Cut out a smaller circle, about 1 cm (½ in), in the middle so you are left with a hollow centre in half of the biscuits. Arrange them all on the lined baking tray and bake for 15–18 minutes until golden brown. If you'd like a biscuit with a bit more of a snap, bake for a few minutes longer.

5. Allow the biscuits to cool completely on the tray, then dust the biscuits with the holes with icing sugar. Pipe a buttercream dam (page 39) around the edges of the bottom biscuits and sandwich the top and bottom biscuits together. Spoon or pipe the jam into the centre of the biscuits. Serve.

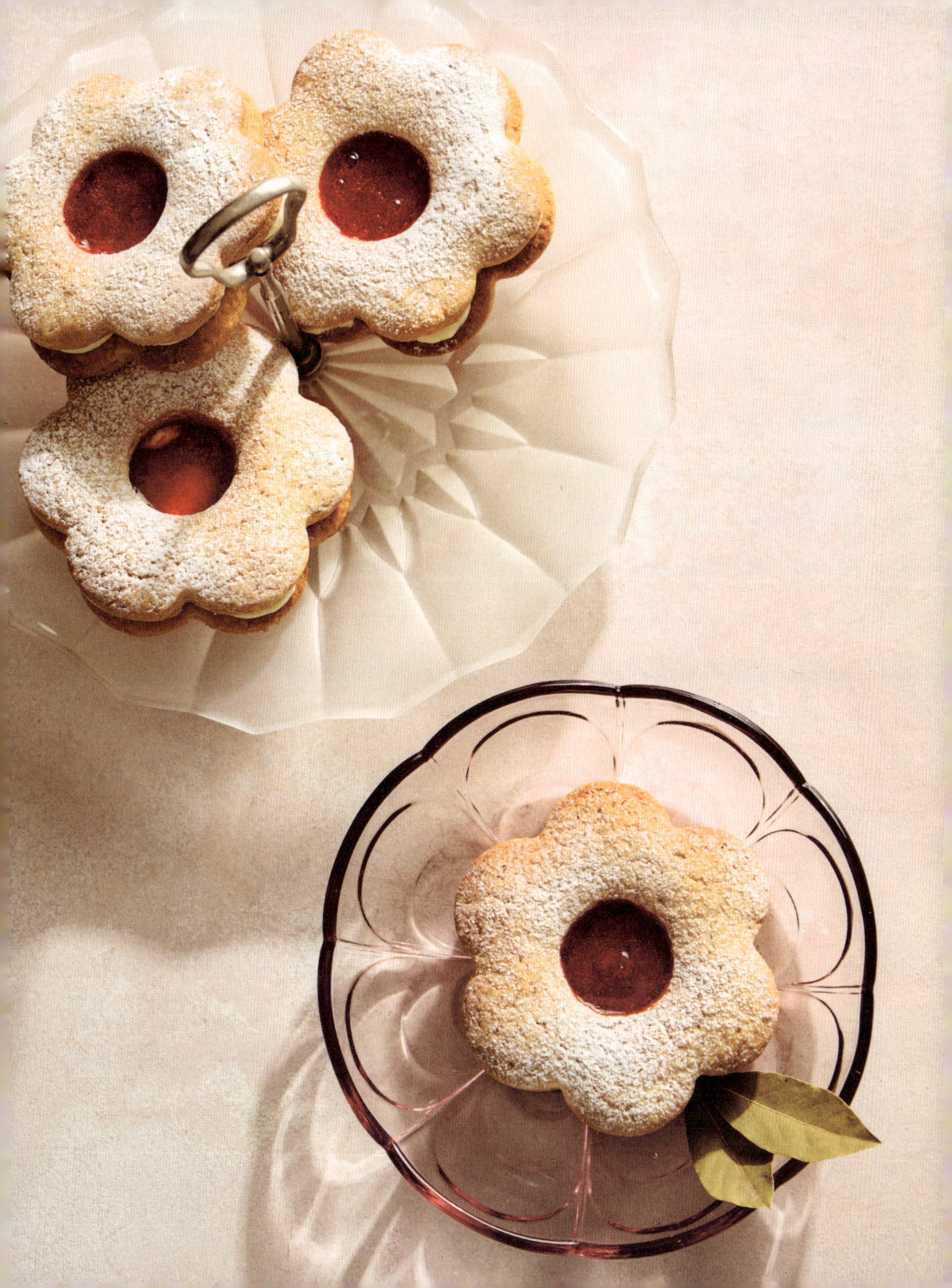

Raspberry Checkerboard Biscuits

Makes about 24 biscuits

These biscuits have a Battenberg-inspired style resulting in a fun biscuit design with subtle hints of raspberry.

---

1 batch of Biscuit dough (page 30)
pink food colouring
plain (all-purpose) flour, for dusting
3 tablespoons granulated sugar
10 g (0.35 oz) freeze-dried raspberry powder, sifted

1 Make a batch of biscuit dough according to the instructions on page 30. Divide it into two, roughly 400 g (14.10 oz) each. Leave one plain and colour the other pink using food colouring and knead until you get your desired colour.

2 Roll out each dough on a lightly floured work surface until it is 1 cm (½ in) thick and a 15 x 15 cm (6 x 6 in) square. Brush a little water on the pink layer, then place the plain layer on top and cut the square in half to create two 7.5 x 15 cm (3 x 6 in) rectangles. Brush more water on one of the rectangles and place the layers on top of each other so that you have four layers alternating plain, pink, plain, pink. Cut 1 cm (½ in) strips lengthways until you have six strips. Then, place a strip down flat on its side so all four layers are showing plain, pink, plain, pink. Then brush with a little water and place the other strip pink, plain, pink, plain. Then repeat for the final layer plain, pink, plain, pink, leaving you with a 12 square alternating pattern. Then repeat with the other 3 strips and wrap the block in clingfilm tightly and chill in the refrigerator for 30 minutes.

3 Preheat the oven to 170°C fan (375°F) and line a baking tray (pan) with baking parchment.

4 Mix the sugar and raspberry powder together in a shallow dish. Slice the chilled dough into 1 cm (½ in) thick blocks and brush the edges with a little water. Roll in the raspberry sugar, then arrange on the prepared baking tray and bake for 10–12 minutes until slightly golden and firm to the touch. Enjoy.

TIP

You can freeze extra biscuit dough and bake from frozen if you only need a few biscuits. Just add a couple of extra minutes to the baking time.

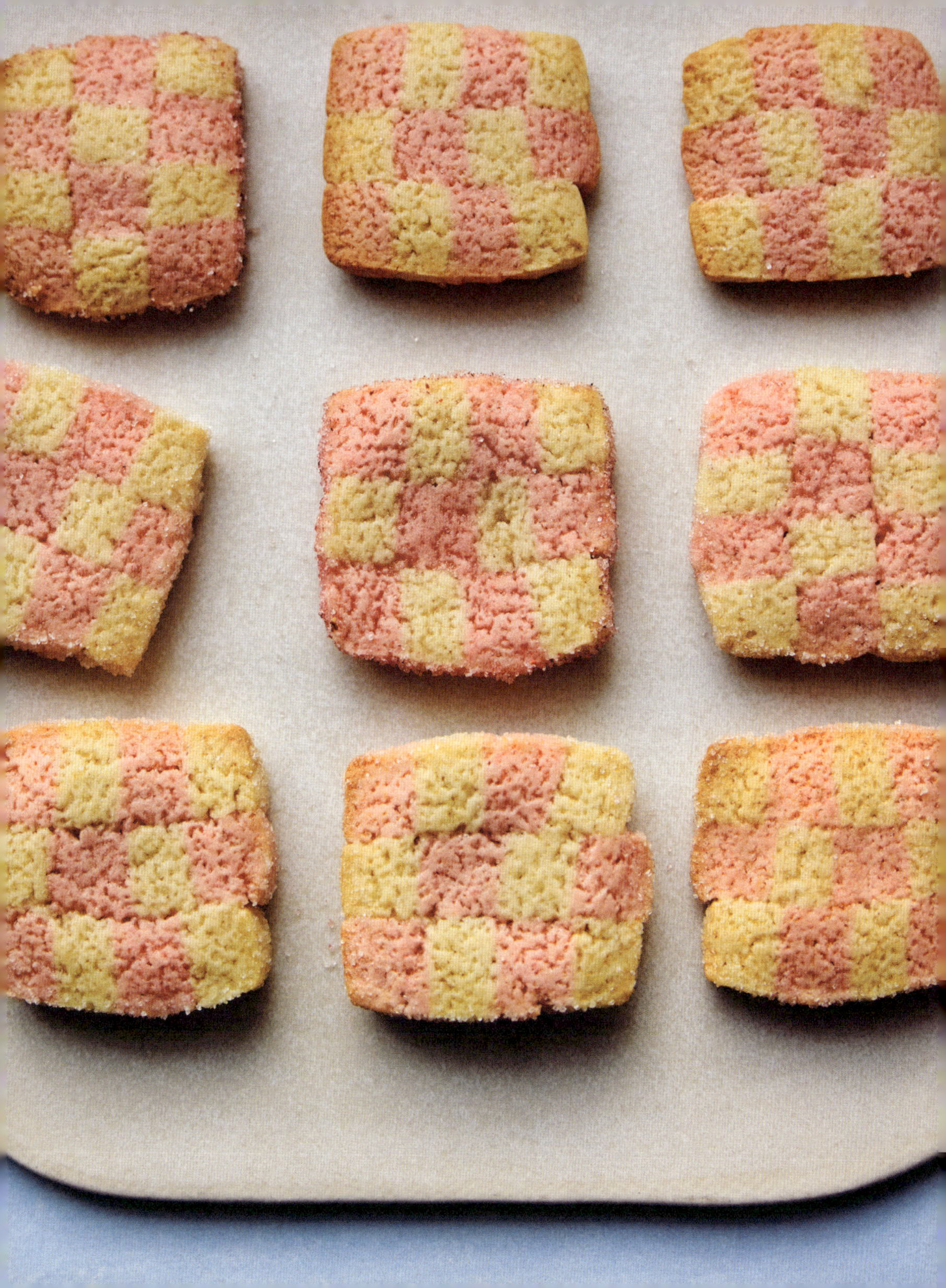

Brown Butter Pumpkin Spice Deep Dish Cookies

Makes 8–9 cookies

These deep-dish cookies combine brown butter, caramelised white chocolate and cinnamon ganache to make for a moreish cookie treat. You will definitely want to eat more than one.

---

non-stick spray or unsalted butter, for greasing
100 g (3.52 oz) cold unsalted butter, cut into cubes
15 g (0.52 oz) cold Brown Butter (page 26)
190 g (6.70 oz) light brown sugar
1 egg, cold
40 g (1.41 oz) pumpkin purée
235 g (8.28 oz) plain (all-purpose) flour
1 tablespoon cornflour (cornstarch)
½ teaspoon bicarbonate of soda (baking soda)
2 tablespoons pumpkin spice blend (see recipe below)
100 g (3.52 oz) Caramelised White Chocolate chunks (page 23)

For the pumpkin spice blend

1 teaspoon ground cinnamon
1 teaspoon ground ginger
1 teaspoon ground nutmeg
1 teaspoon ground cloves
1 teaspoon ground allspice

For the white chocolate cinnamon ganache

75 g (2.64 oz) white chocolate
75 g (2.64 oz) double (heavy) cream
1 teaspoon ground cinnamon

1. Preheat the oven to 170°C fan (375°F) and grease a 12-hole muffin tin (pan).

2. Mix all the spices for the pumpkin spice blend in a small bowl and set aside.

3. Mix the butters and sugar together in a large bowl either with a wooden spoon or a hand mixer until combined. Add the egg and pumpkin purée and beat again until just combined. Don't overmix.

4. Add the flour, cornflour, bicarbonate of soda and pumpkin spice blend and beat using a mixer to begin to incorporate. Add the caramelised chocolate and mix until a soft cookie dough forms.

5. Form the dough into 80 g (2.82 oz) balls and push them into the prepared muffin tin. Bake for 12–14 minutes until golden brown with a slightly soft centre. While the cookies are still warm, use a small spoon or cup to press an indentation into the cookies, then leave in the tin for 5 minutes. Tip onto a wire rack and allow to cool completely.

6. For the ganache, melt the white chocolate in the cream, then add the cinnamon. Pour the ganache into the dip in each cookie and allow to set until your desired consistency. Store in an airtight container for up to two days.

TIP
You can freeze extra cookie dough in portions and cook at any time. Just add a couple of extra minutes to the baking time.

Lemon & Blueberry Crumble Cookies

Makes 8–9

Crumble pieces plus cookie dough, yes please! These are quite sweet yet have a nice contrast with the tanginess of the lemon and sharp blueberries.

---

115 g (4.5 oz) cold unsalted butter, cut into cubes
190 g (6.70 oz) light brown sugar
zest of 1 lemon
1 egg, cold
235 g (8.28 oz) plain (all-purpose) flour
1 tablespoon cornflour (cornstarch)
½ teaspoon bicarbonate of soda (baking soda)
50 g (1.76 oz) blueberries, fresh or frozen

For the crumble topping

50 g (1.76 oz) packed light or dark brown sugar
25 g (0.88 oz) granulated sugar
1 teaspoon cinnamon
½ teaspoon salt
55 g (1.94 oz) unsalted butter, melted
100 g (3.52 oz) plain (all-purpose) flour

1. Preheat the oven to 170°C fan (375°F) and line a baking tray (pan) with baking parchment.

2. For the crumble topping, mix both sugars, the cinnamon and salt together in a medium bowl. Stir in the melted butter, then gently mix in the flour with a fork. Keep the mixture as large crumbles and do not overmix. If overmixed, it will turn into a thick paste. Store in the refrigerator until needed.

3. Add the butter, light brown sugar and lemon zest to a large bowl and beat with an electric mixer until combined. Add the egg and beat again until combined. Add the flour, cornflour and bicarbonate of soda and beat on low speed to begin to incorporate. Just when the dough is forming, add the blueberries so they don't get too squished.

4. Form the dough into 90 g (3.17 oz) balls. Try to handle the dough as little as possible, then roll the cookies in the crumble mix and arrange four to five on the prepared baking tray, spaced well apart as they will spread during baking.

5. Bake for 12–14 minutes until golden brown. Enjoy warm or allow to cool completely on the tray. Best eaten the same day.

TIP

Frozen blueberries work better as they keep their shape more and don't bleed into the dough.

COOKIES & BISCUITS

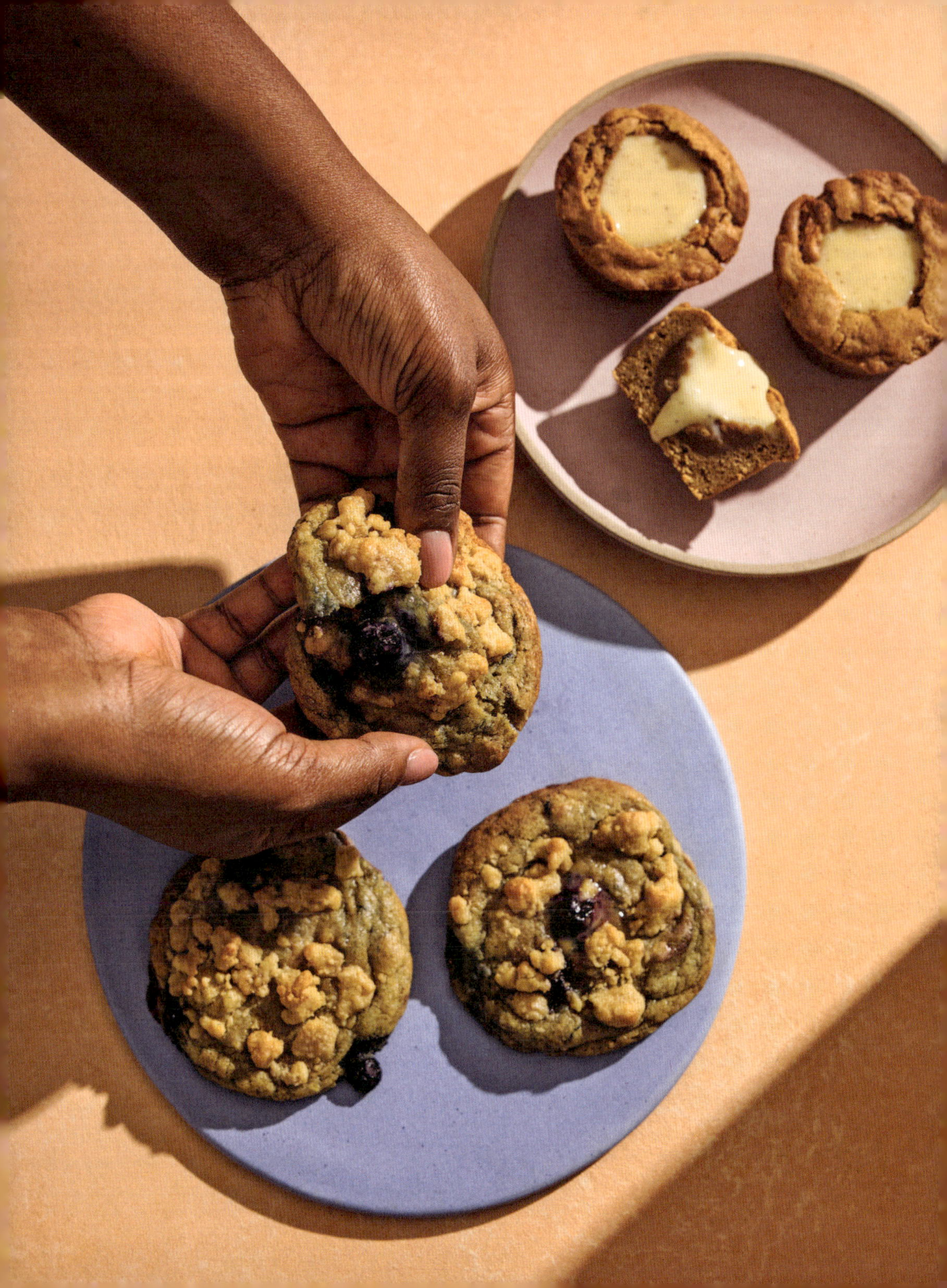

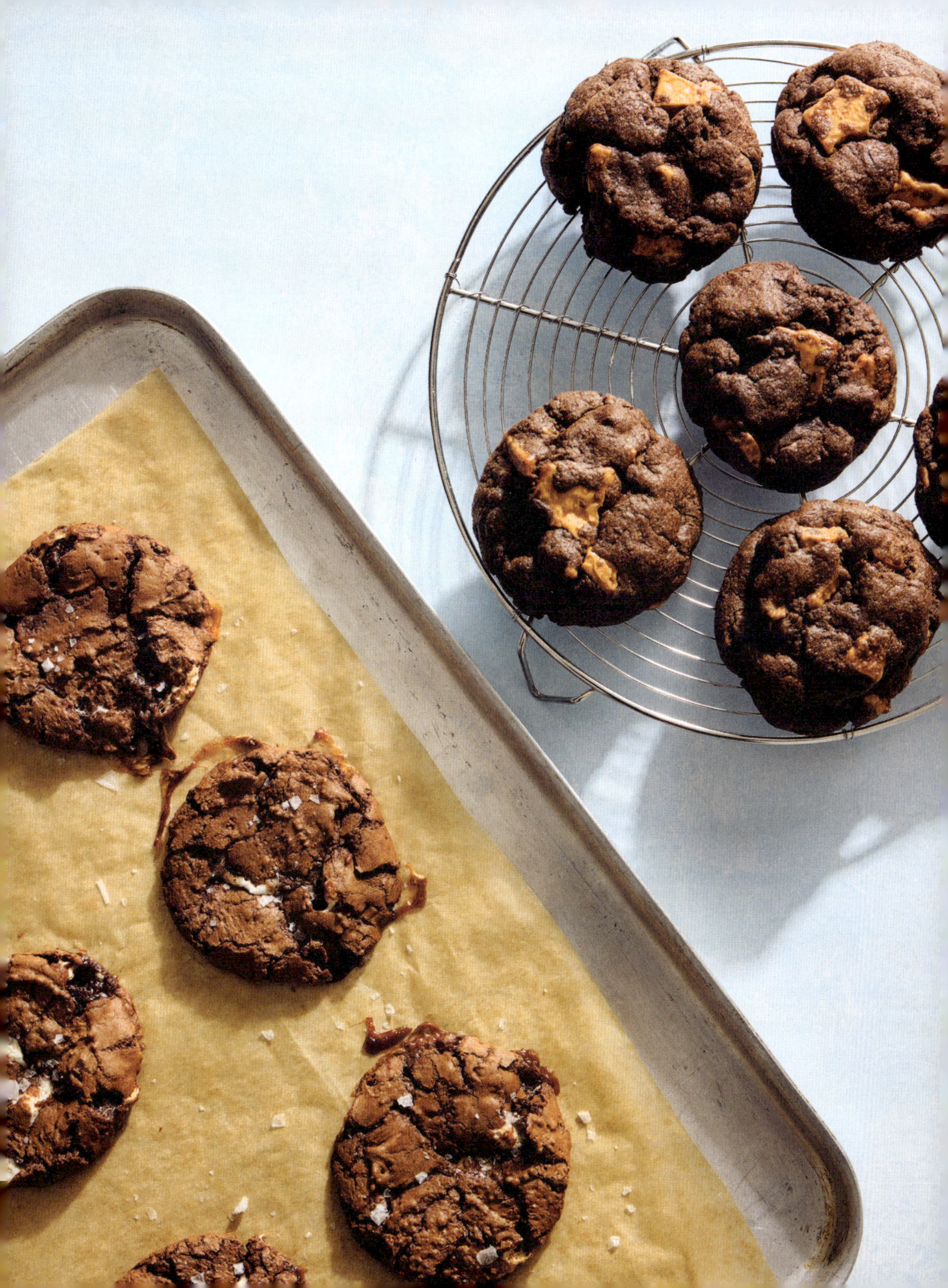

Chocolate & Caramelised White Chocolate Cookies

Makes 8–9 cookies

These are classic chocolate cookies but instead of milk or dark chocolate chips I've used caramelised white chocolate to give a caramel nutty hint to the cookies.

- 115 g (4.05 oz) cold unsalted butter, cut into cubes
- 190 g (6.70 oz) light brown sugar
- 1 egg, cold
- 235 g (8.28 oz) plain (all-purpose) flour
- 1 tablespoon cornflour (cornstarch)
- ½ teaspoon bicarbonate of soda (baking soda)
- 30 g (1.05 oz) cocoa (unsweetened chocolate) powder, sifted
- 100 g (3.52 oz) Caramelised White Chocolate chunks (page 23)

1. Preheat the oven to 170°C fan (375°F) and line two baking trays (pans) with baking parchment.

2. Add the butter and sugar to a large bowl and beat with an electric mixer until combined. Add the egg and beat again until combined. Add the flour, cornflour, bicarbonate of soda and cocoa powder and beat on low speed to begin to incorporate, then add the caramelised chocolate and mix until a soft cookie dough forms.

3. Form the dough into 90 g (3.17 oz) balls and gently squeeze the dough together. Don't roll them in your hands so they remain chunky when baked.

4. Place four to five balls on each of the prepared baking trays so they have room to spread a little and bake for 12–14 minutes until the edges are firm to the touch but the centre still has some softness. Enjoy warm or leave them to cool completely on the tray. Store in an airtight container for up to four days.

TIP

You can also make these ahead of time and freeze any extra dough balls you have, then bake from frozen. Just add a couple extra minutes of baking time.

Brownie S'mores Cookies

Makes 6 cookies

These cookies are very fudgy and the addition of marshmallows gives you a s'more-like brownie in cookie form. What's not to love?

- 65 g (2.29 oz) unsalted butter, cut into cubes
- 100 g (3.52 oz) dark chocolate (at least 70% cocoa solids), broken into pieces
- 1 egg
- 75 g (2.64 oz) caster (superfine) sugar
- 50 g (1.76 oz) light brown sugar
- 65 g (2.29 oz) plain (all-purpose) flour
- 1 teaspoon baking powder
- 1 tablespoon cocoa (unsweetened powder) powder, sifted
- ½ teaspoon salt, plus extra for sprinkling
- 30 g (1.05 oz) small marshmallows

1. Preheat the oven to 170°C fan (375°F) and line a large baking tray (pan) with baking parchment.

2. Melt the butter and chocolate in a heatproof bowl in the microwave. Set aside.

3. Whisk the egg and both sugars together in a large bowl until pale and fluffy, then fold in the melted butter and chocolate mixture.

4. Add the dry ingredients together with the marshmallows and fold in until everything is fully combined. Using an ice-cream scoop or two spoons, scoop the batter (about 50 g/1.76 oz) at a time) onto the prepared baking tray, spaced well apart as the cookies will spread during baking. Sprinkle a little extra salt on top, then bake for 10–12 minutes. They will be done when the edges are firm but the centre is still a little soft.

5. Allow the cookies to fully cool on the tray as they'll initially be quite soft. Store in an airtight container for up to four days.

Lavender Shortbread

Makes 8–10 biscuits

These classic shortbreads have a lavender infusion, which is simple yet effective.

---

125 g (4.40 oz) cold unsalted butter, cut into cubes
55 g (1.94 oz) caster (superfine) sugar, plus extra for sprinkling
2 teaspoons lavender buds
180 g (6.34 oz) plain (all-purpose) flour, plus extra for dusting

1. Preheat the oven to 170°C fan (375°F) and line a baking tray (pan) with baking parchment.

2. Mix the butter, sugar and lavender together in a large bowl until combined. Add the flour and mix until a dough comes together.

3. Roll the dough out on a lightly floured work surface into a long log, about 25 cm (10 in) long, then wrap in cling film (plastic wrap) and chill in the refrigerator for 30 minutes.

4. Slice the chilled dough into 2.5 cm (1 in) thick circles, sprinkle with caster sugar and arrange on the prepared baking tray.

5. Bake for 15–20 minutes until pale golden brown. Set aside to cool on a wire rack. Store in an airtight container for up to a week.

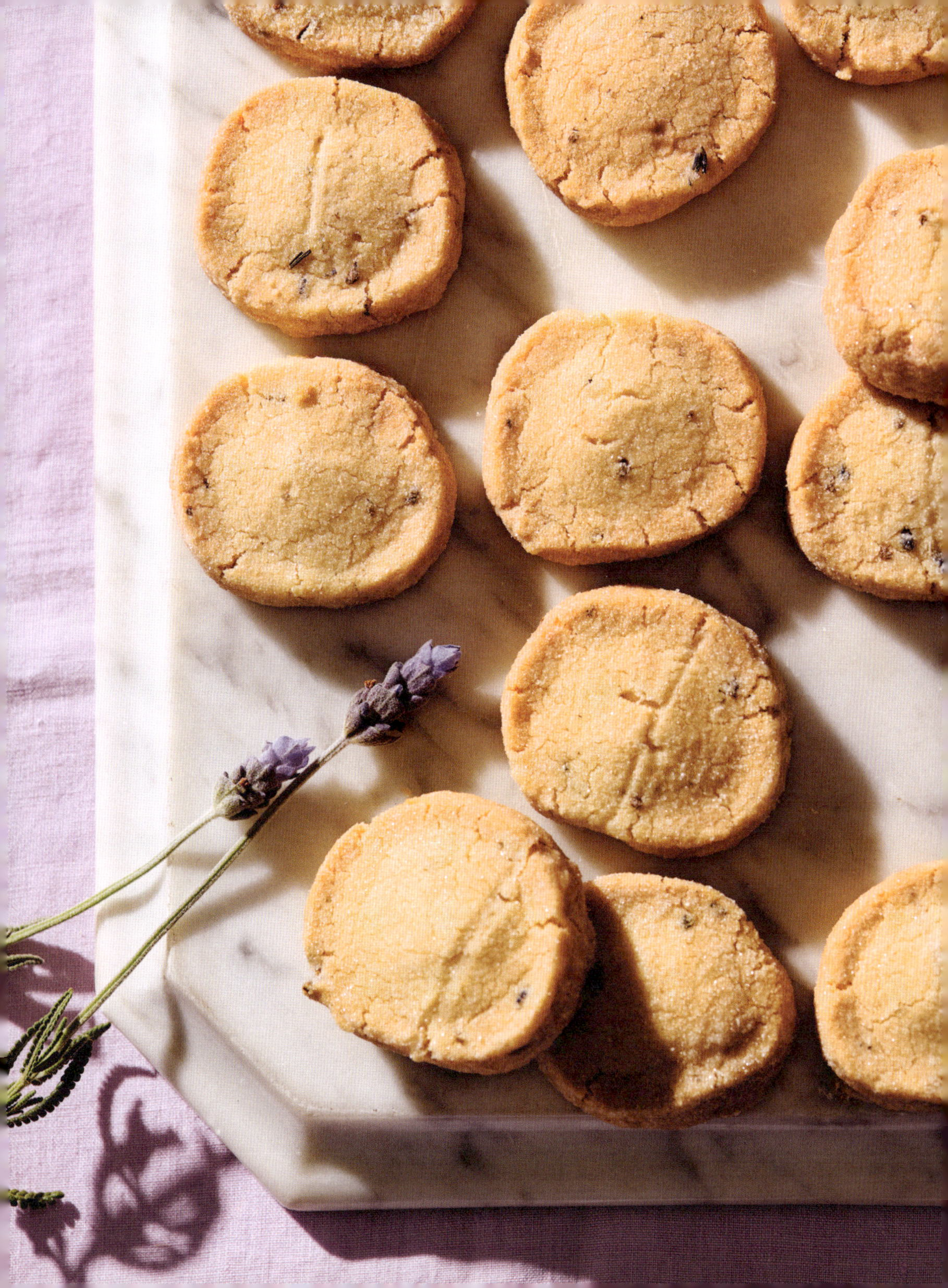

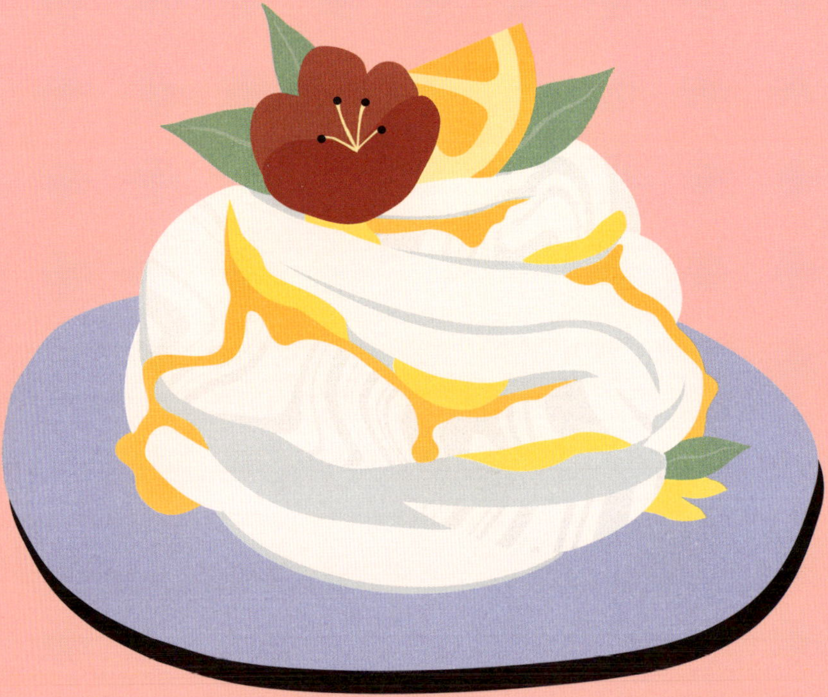

Desserts

This chapter combines different components to create delicious showstopping desserts. It has a bit of everything, something fruity, something chocolatey, with recipes that are achievable and creative. The recipes are also adaptable so you can put your own twist on flavour combinations and try something new.

Mango & Lemon Pavlova / 82

Madeleines Banana Pudding / 84

Brownie with Espresso Whipped Cream / 86

Birthday Cake Blondies / 87

Crème Brûlée Basque Cheesecake / 90

Black Forest Tiramisu / 92

Raspberry & Pistachio Trifle / 94

Earl Grey & Blackberry Coulis Blancmange / 96

Mango & Lemon Pavlova

Serves about 6

Mango is my favourite fruit so making a curd with it is a delicious way to give a tropical vibe to a pavlova.

For the meringue

2 egg whites
110 g (3.88 oz) caster (superfine) sugar
½ teaspoon cornflour (cornstarch), sifted

For the lemon and mango curd

½ mango (about 50 g/1.76 oz), peeled, stoned and cut into slices
2 egg yolks, beaten
100 g (3.52 oz) caster (superfine) sugar
zest and juice of 1 lemon
60 g (2.02 oz) unsalted butter

For the cream filling

200 g (7.05 oz) double (heavy) cream
50 g (1.76 oz) icing (confectioners') sugar
1 teaspoon vanilla paste

To decorate

mango slices
edible flowers

1. Preheat the oven to 110°C fan (275°F).

2. To make the meringue, whisk the egg whites in an electric mixer until just before stiff peaks form. Alternatively, use a bowl and a hand whisk. While whisking constantly, add the sugar, a tablespoon at a time, until thick, glossy and the sugar dissolves. Fold in the sifted cornflour until incorporated.

3. Draw a 10 cm (4 in) and 15 cm (6 in) circle spaced out on a sheet of baking parchment, then turn the parchment over and place it on a baking tray (pan). Depending on the size of your tray you may need two baking trays with a circle drawn on each one. Spoon the meringue over the circles and flatten slightly. Bake for 20 minutes, then reduce the oven temperature to 90°C fan (225°F) and cook for a further 40 minutes, or until crisp and dry. Turn off the oven and leave the meringue in the oven, with the door ajar, for 3–4 hours until cooled completely.

4. For the curd, blend the mango in a blender or food processor until smooth. In a small saucepan over a medium heat, add the egg yolks, sugar, lemon zest and juice and mango purée and whisk constantly for 3–4 minutes, until the mixture is thick enough to coat the back of your spoon. Remove from the heat and, while stirring constantly, add the butter so it is incorporated into the mixture. Strain the curd through a sieve (fine mesh strainer) and allow to cool completely.

5. Using a hand mixer, whip the cream, icing sugar and vanilla together in a large bowl until stiff peaks form. Spoon some of the cream and curd onto the larger meringue circle, then stack the smaller circle on top, spooning more curd and cream on top to construct the pavlova. Decorate with sliced mango and edible flowers.

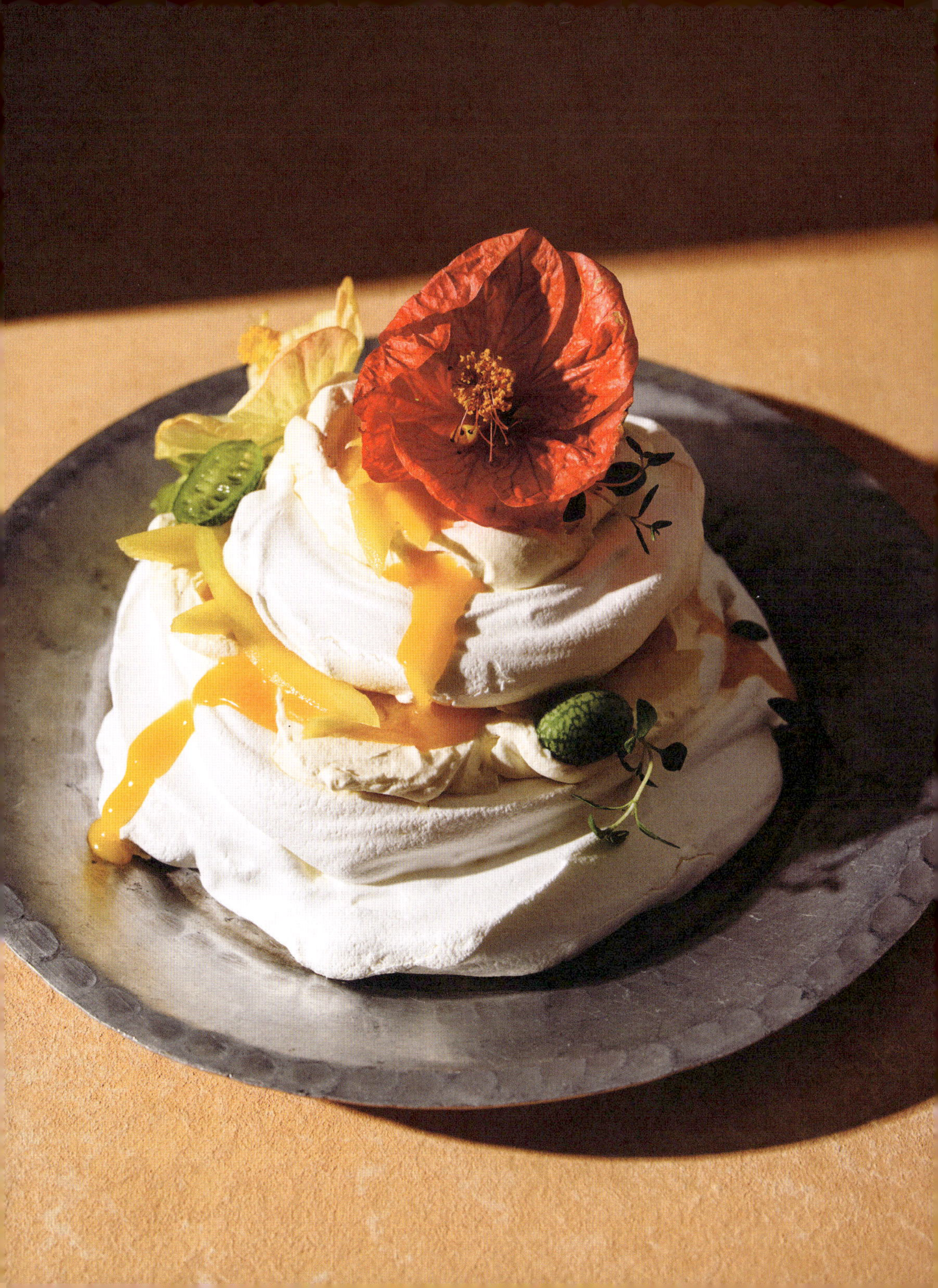

Madeleines Banana Pudding

Serves 4

This is my take on the famous banana pudding, which I tested with madeleines. It worked really well and is a great substitute for the traditional wafers that are usually used in this pudding.

---

1 batch of Vanilla Madeleines (page 42)
85 g (2.99 oz) double (heavy) cream
2 bananas, sliced

For the custard
(about 200 g/7.05 oz)

140 ml (4.73 fl oz) whole milk
1 egg yolk
15 g (0.52 oz) cornflour (cornstarch)
35 g (1.23 oz) caster (superfine) sugar
15 g (0.52 oz) cold unsalted butter, cut into cubes
5 drops (1 teaspoon) banana essence (optional)

For the milk soak

100 g (3.52 oz) whole milk
10 g (0.35 oz) caster (superfine) sugar

1. Make the madeleines according to the instructions on page 42.

2. For the custard, in a saucepan, bring the milk to a low simmer, just before it comes to the boil. Meanwhile, mix the egg yolk, cornflour and sugar together in a large bowl and set aside.

3. Once the milk is hot pour a small amount, about 3 tablespoons into the egg and sugar mixture and whisk together. Don't add the milk all at once otherwise you could cook the eggs and end up with scrambled egg pieces in the custard.

4. While whisking, slowly pour the rest of the milk into the egg and sugar mixture until fully combined. Pour the mixture back into the pan and heat over a medium–low heat, stirring constantly, until the mixture thickens and it coats the back of the spoon to the point where you can draw a line through it with your spoon and it holds its shape.

5. Stir in the cold butter all at once until melted, then add the banana essence. Pour the custard into a heatproof bowl and cover the surface of the custard with cling film (plastic wrap) to prevent it forming a skin. Once it has cooled down, store in the refrigerator until required.

6. When ready to assemble the dessert, have a medium-sized serving bowl ready.

7. Using a hand mixer, whip the double cream in a medium bowl until stiff peaks form, then fold in 100 g (3.52 oz) of the custard. Set aside.

8. Make the milk soak by mixing the milk and sugar together in a bowl. Dip the madeleines into the milk soak to soften slightly.

9 Then arrange a layer of them in the bottom of the serving bowl. Pour over some banana custard, then add a layer of bananas, followed by a layer of the cream, and repeat until all the ingredients have been used (save a few banana slices for the top). Chill in the refrigerator for 1 hour before serving.

DESSERTS 85

Brownie *with* Espresso Whipped Cream

Makes 4 squares

These classics flavours of chocolate and coffee create a decadent tiramisu-style brownie.

---

non-stick spray or unsalted butter, for greasing
1 egg
90 g (3.17 oz) caster (superfine) sugar
60 g (2.02 oz) unsalted butter
100 g (3.52 oz) dark chocolate (at least 70% cocoa solids), broken into pieces
60 g (2.02 oz) plain (all-purpose) flour
cocoa (unsweetened chocolate) powder, for dusting

For the espresso cream

200 g (7.05 oz) double (heavy) cream
2 tablespoons strong coffee, cooled
50 g (1.76 oz) icing (confectioners') sugar

1. Preheat the oven to 160°C fan (350°F). Grease and line a 15 cm (6 in) cake tin (pan) with baking parchment.

2. Break the egg into a large bowl, add the caster sugar and give it a few whisks with a hand whisk or electric mixer, then set aside. This helps the sugar start to dissolve.

3. Melt the butter and 70 g (2.46 oz) of the chocolate in a microwavable bowl in the microwave. Stir until melted.

4. Whisk the egg and sugar a little more until the mixture turns paler, then add the chocolate mixture and mix to a smooth paste. Sift in the flour and stir until it is fully combined. Finally, stir in the remaining 30 g (1.05 oz) chocolate pieces. Pour the mixture into the prepared tin and level the top with a spatula or palette knife.

5. Bake for 22–25 minutes until the centre has a slight jiggle to it and the edges are firm. Remove from the oven and allow to cool completely in the tin in the refrigerator for at least 2 hours. The brownie should have a soft centre and fudgy appearance when cooled.

6. For the espresso cream, stir the cream and coffee together in a medium bowl, then add the icing sugar and, using a hand whisk, whip until it thickens and holds its shape.

7. Once the brownie is completely cooled, remove it from the tin and cut into four squares. Spread the espresso cream on top and finish with a dusting of cocoa powder.

Birthday Cake Blondies

Makes 4 squares

These blondies are straightforward and delicious. With the addition of fun sprinkles a great pop of colour is achieved.

---

non-stick spray or unsalted butter, for greasing
115 g (4.05 oz) soft light brown sugar
1 egg
45 g (1.58 oz) Browned Butter (page 26)
¼ teaspoon baking powder
90 g (3.17 oz) plain (all-purpose) flour
60 g (2.02 oz) white chocolate chips
25 g (0.88 oz) sprinkles (your choice but make sure they're bake stable), plus extra for the top
½ teaspoon almond extract (optional)

To decorate

buttercream of your choice (pages 18–21)
4 maraschino cherries

1. Preheat the oven to 170°C fan (375°F) and grease and line a 15 cm (6 in) square tin (pan) with baking parchment.

2. Mix the sugar and egg together in a large bowl until slightly pale. Melt the butter according to the instructions on page 26, then set aside to cool.

3. In another bowl, stir the baking powder, flour, white chocolate chips and sprinkles together, then add to the sugar and egg. Add the melted butter and almond extract (if using) and stir until combined. Pour the batter into the prepared tin and scatter the top with some more sprinkles.

4. Bake for 20–22 minutes until golden brown and the edges are firm with a slight wobble in the centre. Remove from the oven and allow to cool completely in the tin in the refrigerator for at least 2 hours. Turn out of the tin and cut into four squares. Decorate them with a swirl of buttercream and a maraschino cherry.

DESSERTS

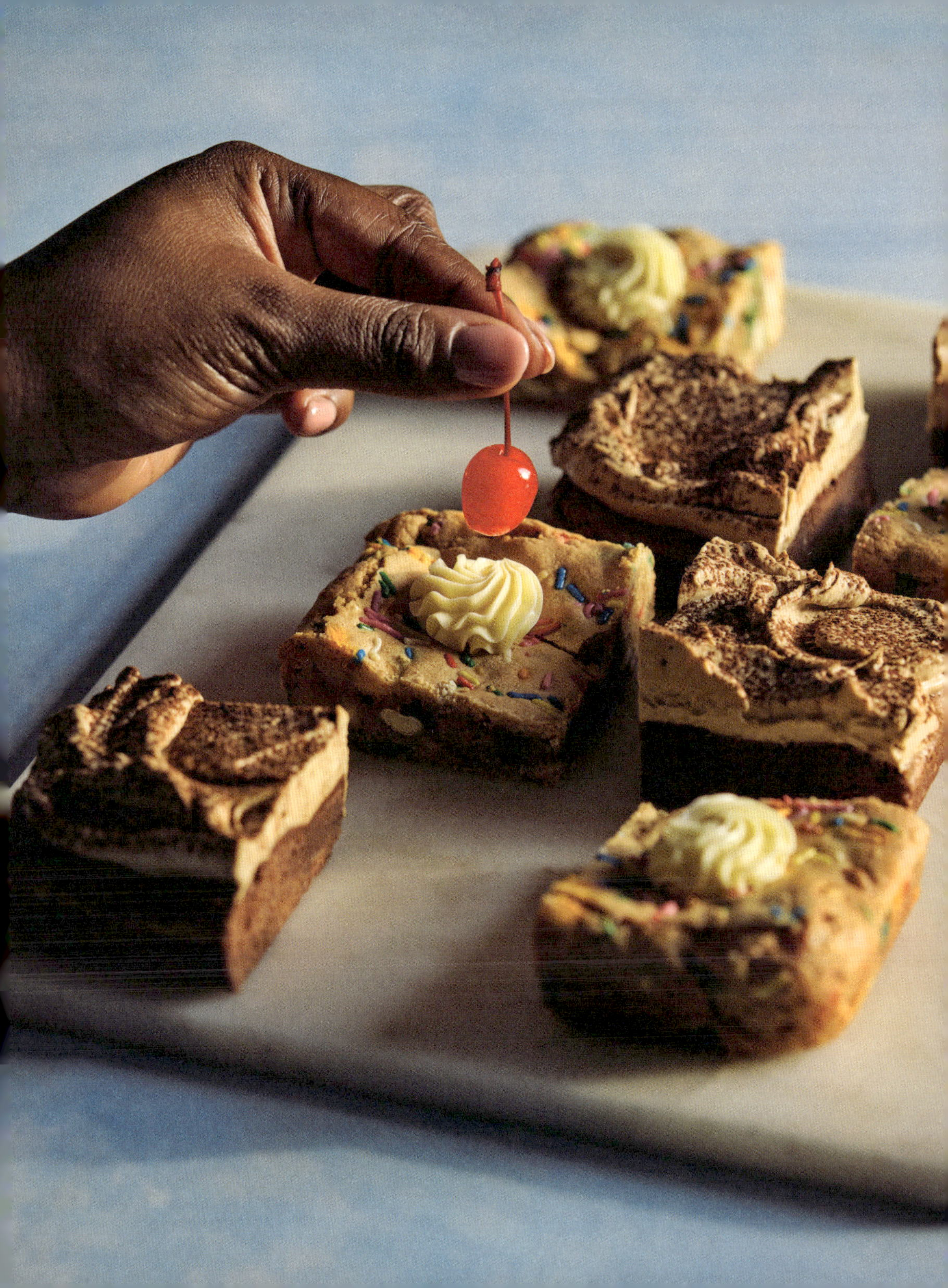

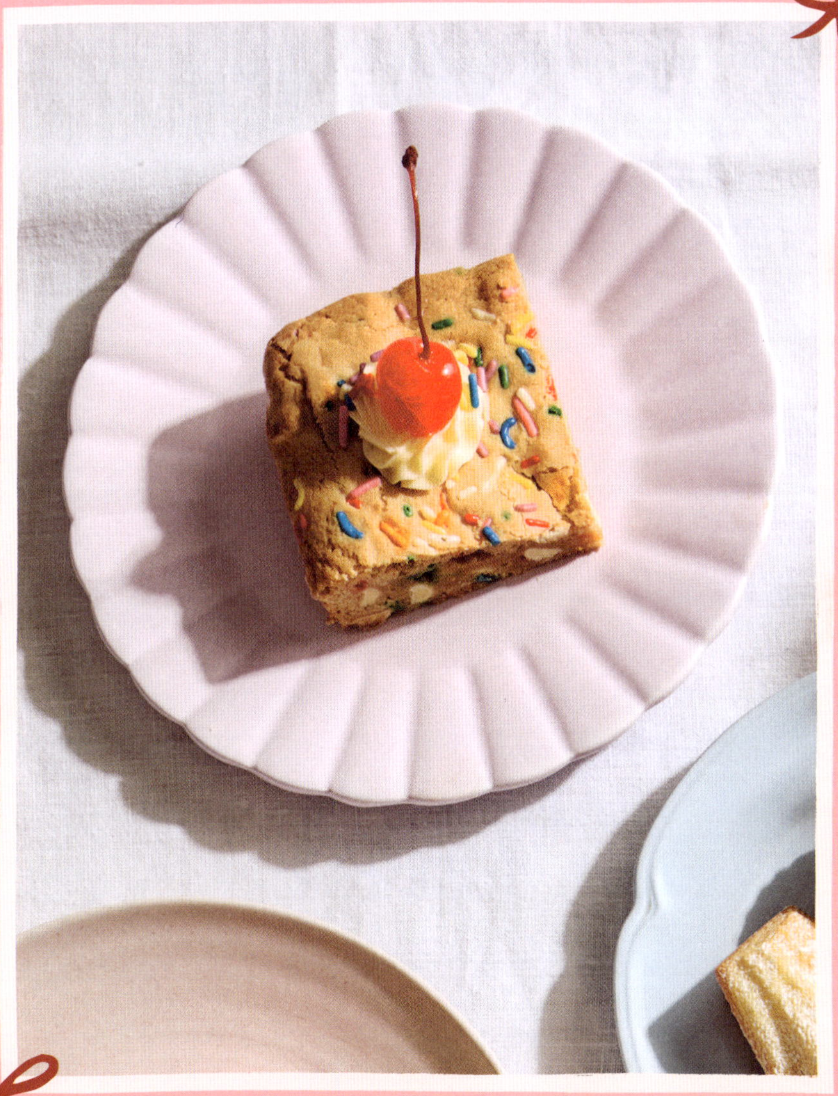

Crème Brûlée
Basque Cheesecake

Serves about 6

Basque cheesecake is such a decadent yet simple dessert to make, but the addition of custard and a brûléed sugar top combines two popular desserts for a very tasty result.

300 g (10.58 oz) cream cheese, at room temperature
110 g (3.88 oz) caster (superfine) sugar, plus 2 tablespoons for the topping
3 eggs
1 teaspoon vanilla paste
1 teaspoon salt
1 tablespoon cornflour (cornstarch)
300 g (10.58 oz) double (heavy) cream, at room temperature

For the base

125 g (4.40 oz) digestive biscuits
50 g (1.76 oz) butter, melted

For the custard

1 egg yolk
15 g (0.52 oz) cornflour (cornstarch)
35 g (1.23 oz) caster (superfine) sugar
140 g (4.93 oz) whole milk
15 g (0.52 oz) cold unsalted butter, cut into cubes
1 tablespoon vanilla bean paste

TIP

If you don't have a blow torch you can leave out the extra sugar on top and enjoy the cheesecake with just the custard.

1. Preheat the oven to 180°C fan (400°F) and line a tall 15 cm (6 in) tin (pan), preferably a springform tin, by cutting a large piece of baking parchment then scrunching it and unscrunching it. Ensure the whole baking parchment is pressed into the tin covering it completely, with some of the parchment hanging over the sides.

2. For the base, blitz the biscuits and melted butter in a food processor. Alternatively, crush the biscuits in a plastic bag with a rolling pin then mix with the melted butter. Spread the biscuit mixture across the bottom of the tin and pat down to firm.

3. For the cheesecake, beat the cream cheese in a large bowl with an electric hand mixer on medium–high speed until very smooth. Alternatively, whisk in a bowl with a balloon whisk. Add the sugar and continue mixing until well combined and the sugar is dissolved with no lumps.

4. Beat in the eggs, one at a time, mixing well before adding the next and scraping down the sides of the bowl between each addition. Beat in the vanilla and salt. In a small bowl, whisk the cornflour and half of the cream together until smooth. Add it to the rest of the batter and mix well. Gradually beat in the remaining cream until combined and the batter is smooth and silky. Pour the batter through a sieve (fine mesh strainer) into the prepared tin.

5. Bake for 30–35 minutes until deeply dark brown on top and still very jiggly in the centre. Transfer the tin to a wire rack and allow to cool completely in the tin, then refrigerate for at least 2 hours, or preferably overnight.

6. To make the custard, whisk the egg yolk, cornflour and sugar in a heatproof bowl. Heat the milk in a saucepan until just before boiling, then pour a small amount of the hot milk into the egg mixture and whisk to incorporate. While mixing, gradually add the rest of the milk, then pour the mixture back into the pan and heat, whisking constantly until the mixture thickens. Once the mixture has thickened, whisk in the cold butter and vanilla. Pour the custard into a large bowl and cover the top with cling film (plastic wrap), ensuring that it touches the surface.

7. Once your cheesecake has chilled, carefully take it out of the tin and peel away the baking parchment. To finish, spoon the custard on top of the cheesecake and sprinkle with the 2 tablespoons caster sugar. Use a blow torch to caramelise the top.

DESSERTS

Black Forest Tiramisu

Serves 4

I love a traditional tiramisu but wanted to give it a little twist by omitting the coffee and replacing it with a hot chocolate mix for dipping the sponge fingers into. Sponge fingers are one of the only things I prefer to buy rather than making them myself; it saves on time as well.

For the cherry curd

- 50 g (1.76 oz) pitted cherries
- 20 ml (0.67 fl oz) water
- 100 g (3.52 oz) caster (superfine) sugar
- 60 g (2.02 oz) unsalted butter
- 2 egg yolks, beaten
- 1 teaspoon almond extract

For the chocolate mix

- 25 g (0.88 oz) cocoa (unsweetened chocolate) powder
- 100 g (3.52 oz) double (heavy) cream
- 50 g (1.76 oz) whole milk
- 25 g (0.88 oz) caster (superfine) sugar
- 2 tablespoons cherry liqueur (optional)

For the mascarpone cream

- 250 g (8.81 oz) mascarpone
- 100 g (3.52 oz) double (heavy) cream
- 25 g (0.88 oz) caster (superfine) sugar

To assemble

- 15 sponge fingers
- cocoa (unsweetened chocolate) powder, for dusting
- fresh cherries, to decorate

1. Start with the cherry curd. Add the pitted cherries to a large saucepan with the water and boil until soft. Transfer the cherries to a blender or food processor and blend until pulped. Add the cherry pulp, sugar and butter to a heatproof bowl set over a pan of simmering water and stir occasionally until the butter has melted. Then, using a small whisk or fork, stir in the egg yolks. Keep gently whisking the mixture over the heat for 10 minutes, or until thickened. Keep stirring so you don't cook the egg yolks and end up with scrambled egg pieces in the curd. Pour the curd through a sieve (fine mesh strainer) into a clean bowl, then stir in the almond extract and allow to cool completely.

2. For the chocolate mix, combine the cocoa powder, cream, milk, sugar and cherry liqueur (if using) in a medium bowl. Mix together until incorporated and set aside.

3. For the mascarpone cream, whisk the mascarpone, cream and sugar together until stiff peaks form.

4. Now you have all the components to construct your tiramisu. First, dip the sponge fingers into the chocolate mix until fully coated, then arrange them in the bottom of a serving dish or bowl. Spoon some of the cherry curd on top, followed by some of the mascarpone cream and repeat until you have a used up all the ingredients. Dust the top with cocoa powder and decorate with fresh cherries.

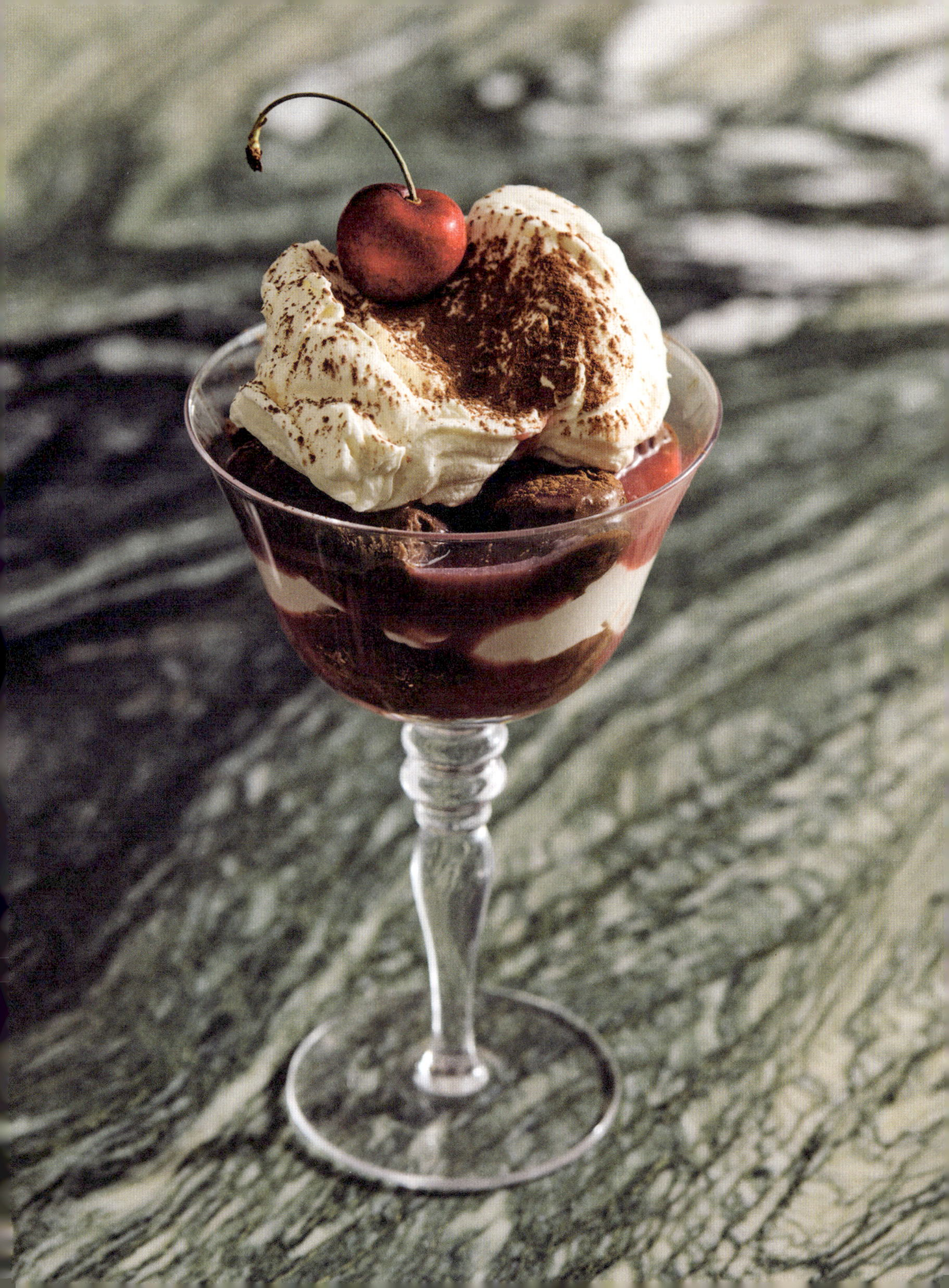

Raspberry & Pistachio Trifle

Serves 5

Trifle is a classic dessert, but I have added a little twist with a pistachio custard for a fun combination. If you don't want to make the jelly then use half a packet of shop-bought jelly.

150 g (5.29 oz) fresh raspberries
35 g (1.23 oz) icing (confectioners') sugar
1 gelatine sheet
150 g (5.29 oz) Custard (page 29)
30 g (1.05 oz) pistachio butter or paste
½ teaspoon green food colouring
100 g (3.52 oz) double (heavy) cream
1 x 15 cm (6 in) Vanilla Cake layer (page 36)

To decorate

fresh raspberries (optional)
chopped pistachios (optional)

1. Bring the raspberries and 25 g (0.88 oz) of the sugar to the boil in a saucepan and boil for 15 minutes. Soak the gelatine sheet in a small bowl of cold water to soften. Pass the raspberry sauce through a sieve (fine mesh strainer) into a bowl, then add the softened gelatine and stir until dissolved. Pour the jelly into a 15 cm (6 in) bowl or dishes you'll be using to serve your trifle and chill in the refrigerator for 2–3 hours. Alternatively, you can make half a packet of shop-bought jelly by following the packet instructions.

2. Make the custard according to the instructions on page 29, adding the pistachio paste and some green food colouring when adding the butter. Allow the custard to cool completely.

3. Meanwhile, using a hand whisk, whip the cream and remaining sugar together in a medium bowl and set aside.

4. Now it's time to assemble. Add the cake on top of the set jelly, then spoon over the pistachio custard and finish with the whipped cream. You can decorate the trifle with fresh raspberries and chopped pistachios.

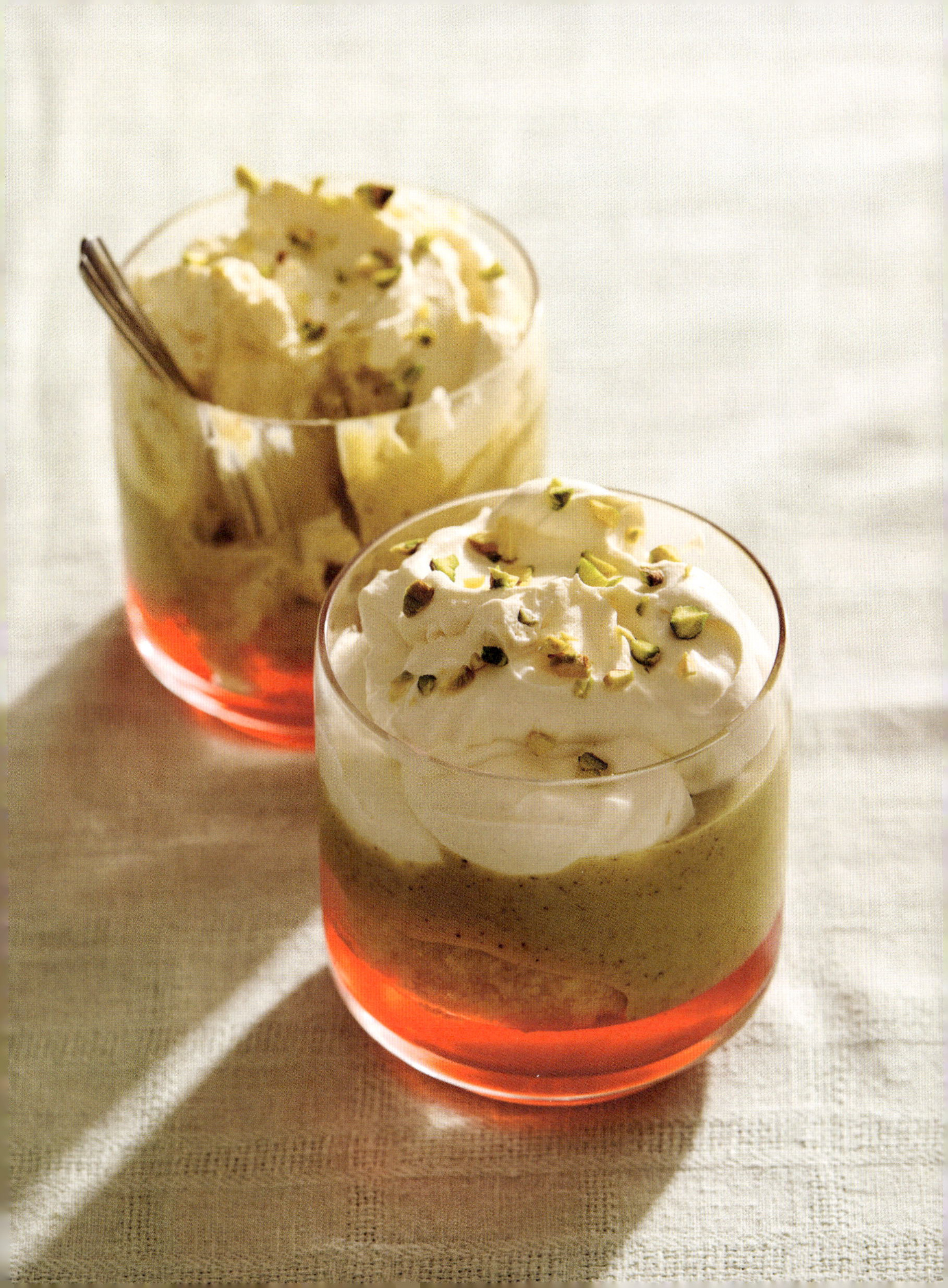

Earl Grey & Blackberry Coulis Blancmange

Makes 2 mini jellies (200 ml/7.05 fl oz moulds)

Blancmange is essentially a milk-based jelly. It's incredibly light with a little sweetness, and the tart blackberries provide a nice contrast.

---

3 gelatine sheets or 1 teaspoon gelatine powder
10 g (0.35 oz) cornflour (cornstarch)
300 g (10.58 oz) whole (full-fat) milk
1 Earl Grey tea bag
75 g (2.64 oz) caster (superfine) sugar
2 fresh blackberries, halved, to decorate (optional)

For the blackberry coulis

50 g (1.76 oz) fresh blackberries
30 g (1.05 oz) caster (superfine) sugar

1. Soak the gelatine sheets in a small bowl of cold water or bloom your powdered gelatine following the packet instructions.

2. Meanwhile, mix the cornflour with 3 tablespoons of the milk in another small bowl until smooth.

3. Add the tea bag to a saucepan along with the remaining milk, sugar and the cornflour mix and bring to the boil. Reduce the heat to medium–low and whisk constantly until the mixture slightly thickens enough to thinly coat the back of a spoon.

4. Squeeze any excess water out of the gelatine, if using sheets, and stir the gelatine into the mixture to dissolve. Set aside to cool for 5 minutes, then pour the mixture into two 200 ml (7.05 fl oz) jelly moulds. Chill in the refrigerator overnight.

5. The next day, make the coulis. Add the blackberries and sugar to a pan and boil for 10 minutes, then remove from the heat and allow to cool before serving.

6. When you're ready to serve, pour some hot water into a large heatproof bowl. Dip each mould into the water, holding it there for 10–20 seconds, then turn the blancmange out onto a serving plate and serve with the coulis and fresh blackberry halves, if you would like.

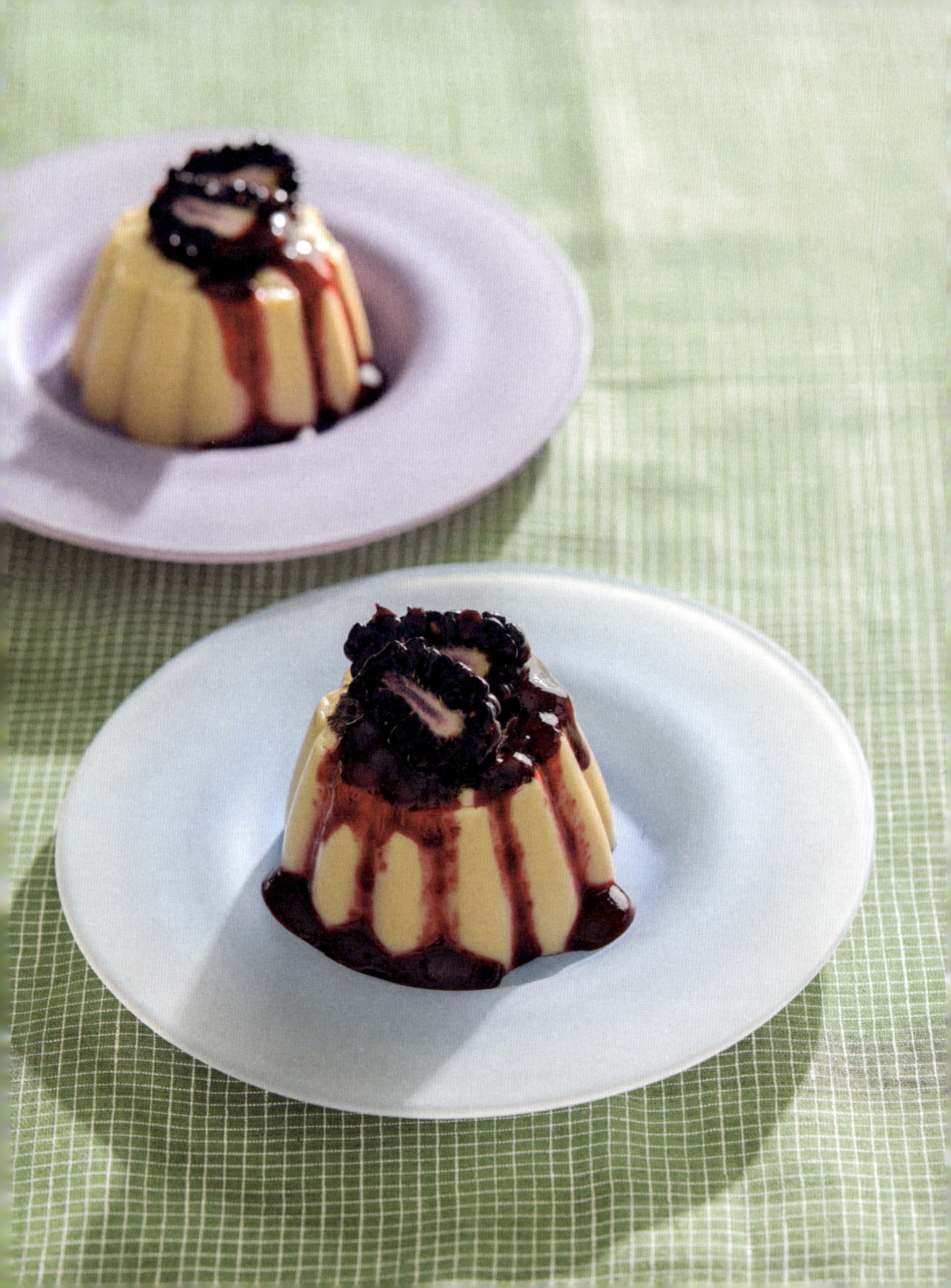

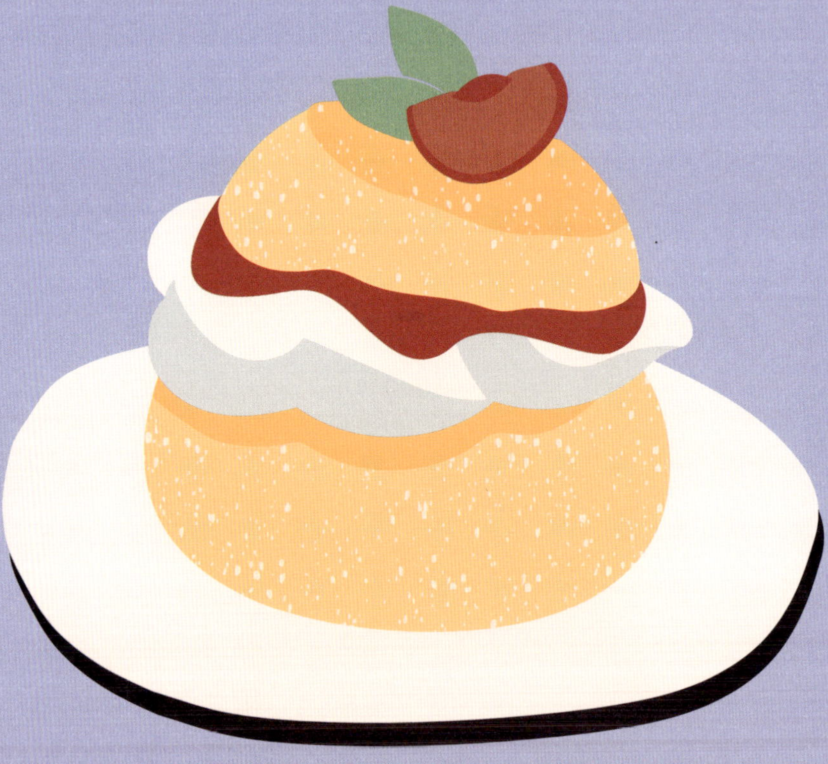

Pastries

Pastries are the perfect blend of simple ingredients and impressive results. In this chapter, you'll find a variety of recipes from buttery tarts to choux pastry in different forms. Don't worry if you find it a little tricky at first – with some practice these recipes will make you feel less intimidated by pastries.

Peach & Cardamom Galette / **102**

Mango & Lime Tarts / **104**

Cherry Bakewell Tart / **106**

Upside-down Banoffee Roll / **107**

Strawberry & Cream Scones / **110**

Plum & Rose Craquelin Choux Buns / **112**

Vanilla & Caramelised
White Chocolate Churros / **114**

Raspberry Custard Buns / **116**

Peach & Cardamom Galette

Serves 6

Peach and cardamom complement each other really well, and this galette is a quick and easy dessert, which is sure to impress. Serve either on its own or with some vanilla ice cream.

---

175 g (6.17 oz) plain (all-purpose) flour, plus extra for dusting
25 g (0.88 oz) icing (confectioners') sugar
100 g (3.52 oz) cold unsalted butter, cut into cubes
1 egg yolk
1 tablespoon cold water

For the frangipane

70 g (2.46 oz) ground almonds
30 g (1.06 oz) light brown sugar
30 g (1.06 oz) caster (superfine) sugar
½ teaspoon salt
15 g (0.52 oz) plain (all-purpose) flour
60 g (2.02 oz) unsalted butter, at room temperature
1 egg
½ teaspoon almond extract
1 teaspoon ground cardamom

For the filling

3 fresh peaches or 1 x 220 g (7.76 oz) tin peaches
2 tablespoons light brown sugar
1 teaspoon ground cardamom

To finish

1 egg, beaten, for egg wash
2 tablespoons caster (superfine) sugar, for sprinkling
icing (confectioners') sugar, for dusting

1. For the pastry, add the flour, icing sugar and butter to a food processor and pulse until crumbly. This can also be done in a bowl by rubbing the butter into the flour with your fingertips until it resembles breadcrumbs. Add the egg yolk and water and pulse until the dough comes together. Wrap the dough in cling film (plastic wrap) and chill in the refrigerator for 2 hours.

2. Preheat the oven to 170°C (375°F). For the frangipane, combine the ground almonds, sugar, salt, flour, butter, egg, almond extract and cardamom in a large bowl or food processor until smooth. Set aside.

3. Cut your peaches into slices or if using tinned peaches, drain and pat dry with paper towels to remove excess moisture.

4. Roll out the chilled dough on a lightly floured work surfce to a 22 cm (9 in) diameter with the thickness of half a centimetre. Spread the frangipane across the rolled-out dough, leaving a 5 cm (2 in) border. Arrange the peaches on top of the frangipane then fold over the edges of the galette, then brush the edges with the egg and sprinkle with the caster sugar. Your galette should be about 18 cm (7 in) once the edges have been rolled inward.

5. Bake for 35–40 minutes until golden brown. While warm, finish with a dusting of icing sugar and serve.

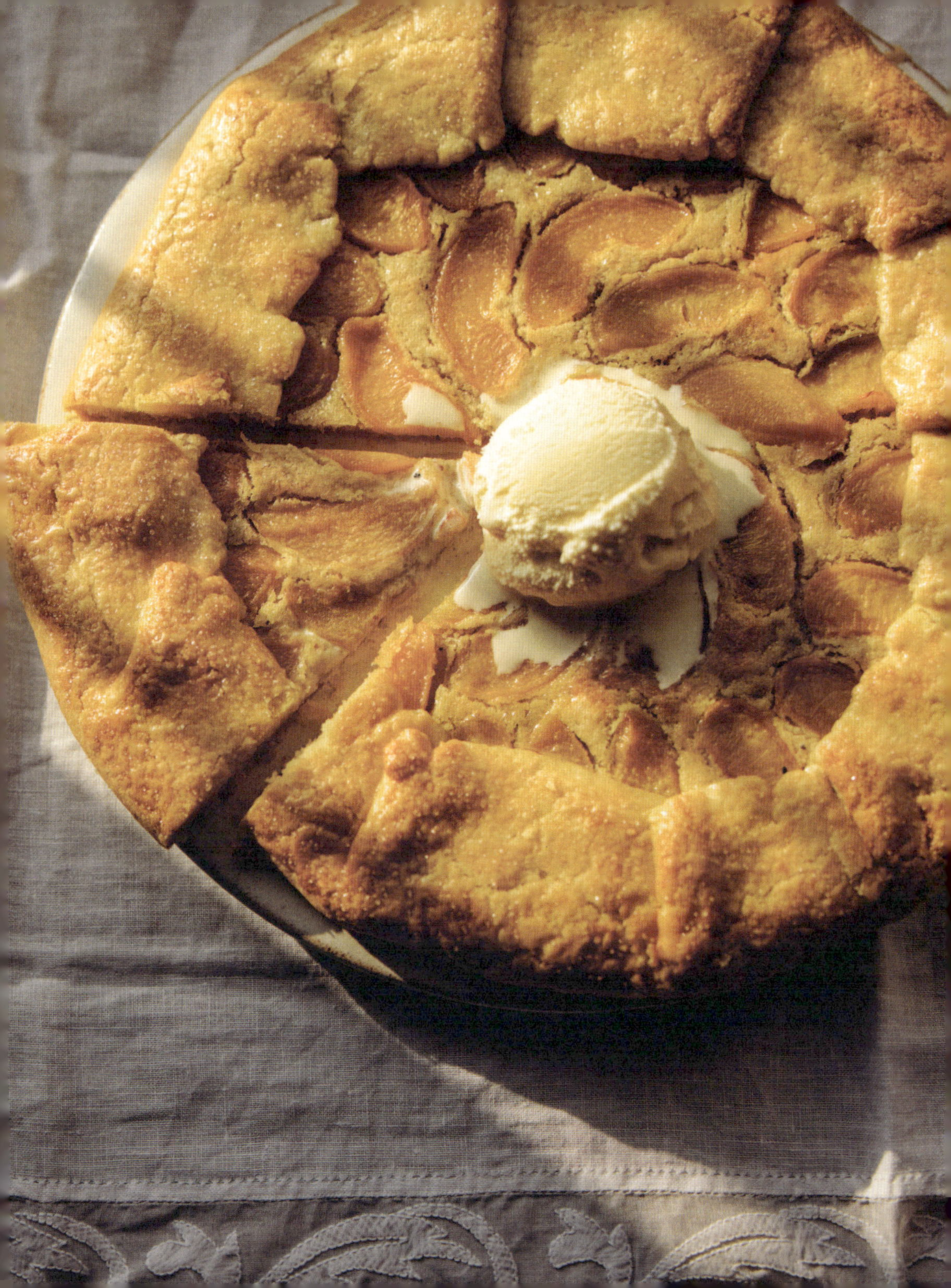

Mango & Lime Tarts

Makes 6–8 tarts

These mini tarts are very simple to make. You can replace the curd with any curd of your choice and even add some whipped cream to the top as well.

---

1 batch of Shortcrust Pastry (page 31)

For the mango and lime curd

pulp from ½ mango (about 50 g/1.76 oz)
zest and juice of 1 lime
100 g (3.52 oz) caster (superfine) sugar
60 g (2.02 oz) butter
2 eggs, beaten

To finish

lime zest
edible flowers

1. Make the shortcrust pastry according to the instructions on page 31. Once the dough has chilled, roll it out until it is 1 cm (½ in) thick, then cut out flower or circle shapes, about 7.5 cm (3 in), and push into the cavities of a muffin tin (pan), ensuring you reach the corners of the tin. Chill in the refrigerator for 30 minutes.

2. For the curd, put the mango pulp, lime zest and juice, sugar and butter in a heatproof bowl set over a saucepan of simmering water. Stir occasionally until the butter has melted. Then, using a small whisk or fork, stir in the beaten eggs. Keep gently whisking the mixture over the heat for 10 minutes, or until thickened. Keep stirring so you don't cook the eggs and end up with scrambled egg pieces. Pour the cooked curd through a sieve (fine mesh strainer) into a clean bowl and set aside.

3. Meanwhile, preheat the oven to 170°C fan (375°F).

4. Prick the bottom of the chilled tarts with a fork, then cover each cavity with baking parchment followed by baking beans. Rice can also be used if you don't have baking beans.

5. Bake for 10 minutes, then remove the baking beans and baking parchment and bake for a further 10 minutes, or until golden brown. Remove from the oven and allow to cool.

6. Once your tart shells are cooled, spoon in the mango and lime curd followed by some lime zest. Decorate with some edible flowers or another decoration of your choice and enjoy.

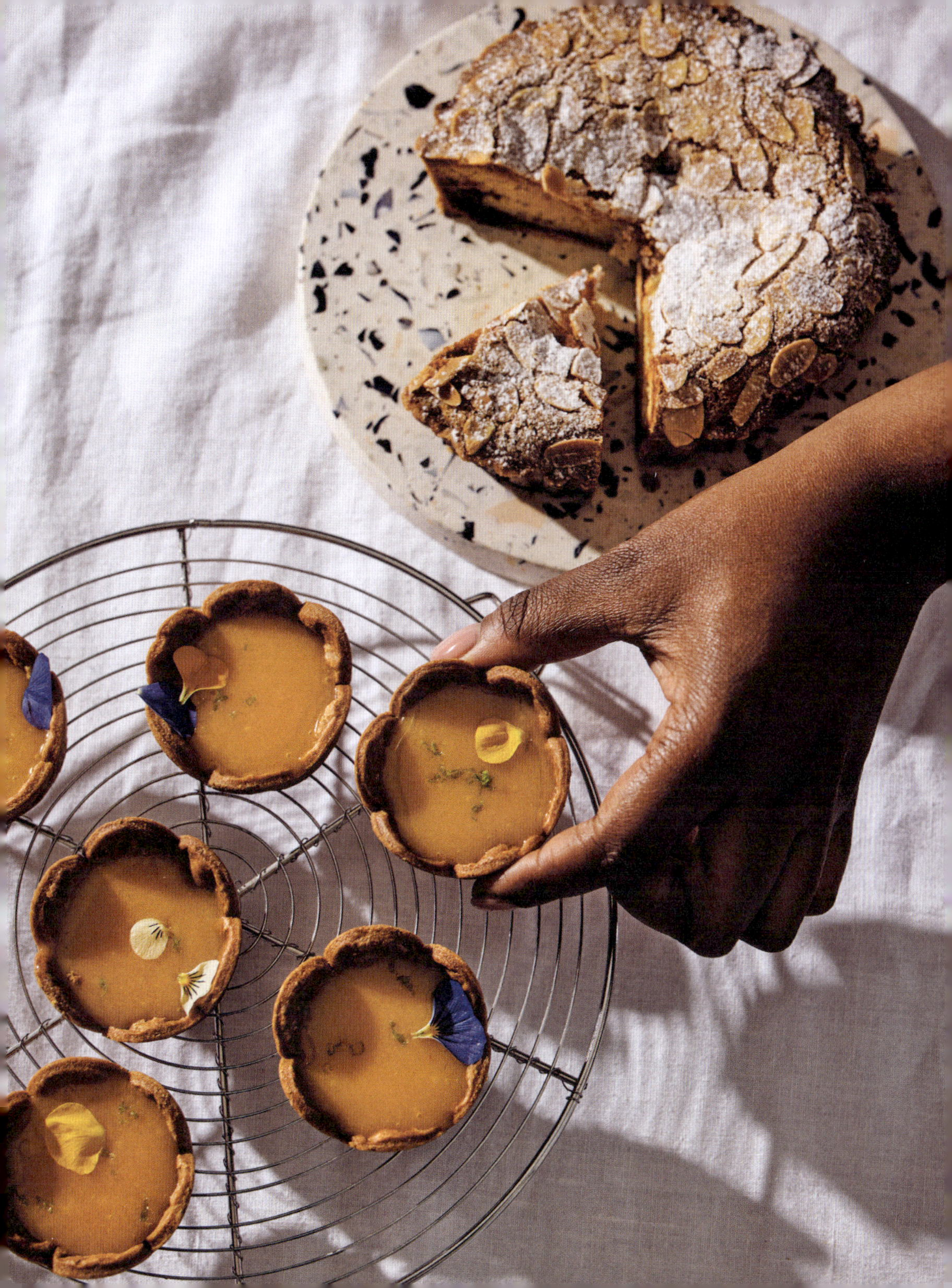

Cherry Bakewell Tart

Serves 4

Cherries and almonds are one of my favourite flavour combinations and in classic tart form you can't go wrong. Pictured on previous page.

---

1 batch of Shortcrust Pastry (page 31)

For the cherry and almond jam

100 g (3.52 oz) cherries, fresh or frozen, pitted
100 g (3.52 oz) caster (superfine) sugar
2 teaspoons almond extract

For the frangipane

120 g (4.23 oz) ground almonds
1 teaspoon almond extract
120 g (4.23 oz) caster (superfine) sugar
100 g (3.52 oz) unsalted butter
10 g (0.35 oz) plain (all-purpose) flour
1 egg
½ teaspoon salt

To finish

flaked (slivered) almonds
icing (confectioners') sugar
double (heavy) cream, whipped

TIP

Leave a little extra pastry around the edges of the tart tin to account for some shrinkage during baking, then use a sharp knife or grater to level the edges.

1. Make the shortcrust pastry according to the instructions on page 31. Once the dough has chilled, roll it out until it is 1 cm (½ in) thick. Roll the pastry onto the a 15 cm (6 in) diameter tart case with a removable base, making sure you reach the corners of the case. Prick the bottom of the tart with a fork and chill in the refrigerator for 30 minutes.

2. Meanwhile, preheat the oven to 170°C fan (375°F).

3. To make the cherry jam, add the pitted cherries and caster sugar to a large saucepan and boil until thickened and soft. Pour the jam into a clean bowl and stir in the almond extract, then set aside.

4. For the frangipane, mix all the ingredients together in a large bowl until smooth. Set aside.

5. Remove the tart from the refrigerator and cover with baking parchment followed by baking beans. Rice can also be used if you don't have baking beans. Bake for 15 minutes, then remove the baking beans and baking parchment and bake for a further 10 minutes, or until golden brown.

6. Spread the cherry and almond jam on the bottom of the baked tart followed by the frangipane, smoothing the top. Sprinkle with flaked almonds. Place the tart back in the oven for 30 minutes, or until the centre is firm and golden brown. Allow the tart to cool completely before removing from the case and slicing. Finish with a dusting of icing sugar and some whipped cream.

Upside-down Banoffee Roll

Serves 6

This recipe combines traditional cinnamon rolls with an upside-down dessert for a fun combo. It's also another way to use up ripe bananas – cut them into discs or even banana halves.

---

non-stick spray or butter,
    for greasing
oil, for greasing
120 g (4.23 fl oz) whole milk
2¼ teaspoons or 7 g packet fast-
    action dried yeast
270 g (9.52 oz) plain flour,
    plus extra for dusting
30 g (1.05 oz) caster (superfine) sugar
¼ teaspoon salt
1 egg
ice cream, to serve (optional)

For the caramel

15 g (0.52 oz) water
50 g (1.76 oz) caster (superfine) sugar
40 g (1.41 oz) double (heavy) cream
15 g (0.52 oz) unsalted butter, cut
    into cubes
1 teaspoon salt, or to taste
1 banana, peeled and cut into slices

For the filling

80 g (2.82 oz) light brown sugar
1 teaspoon ground cinnamon
1 teaspoon cornflour (cornstarch)
80 g (2.82 oz) butter, room
    temperature

1   Grease a 20 cm (8 in) tin (pan) with some non-stick spray or butter and lightly oil a large bowl. In a heatproof bowl, heat the milk until warm to the touch. Test the temperature by dipping your finger in the milk – it should feel a little warmer than room temperature. If it's too hot, leave it to cool for 2 minutes.

2   In a large bowl mix together the flour, sugar, salt and yeast until combined. Pour the milk and egg into the bowl and mix until it all comes together and forms a sticky soft dough that pulls away from the sides of the bowl. This will take around 5 minutes.

3   If doing this by hand I'd recommend kneading your dough on a lightly floured surface for around 5 minutes, until a smooth and soft dough forms. This can also be done in a stand mixer with the dough hook attachment, so you don't need to knead the dough. Shape the dough into a ball and put it into the oiled bowl.

4   Cover with cling film (plastic wrap) and leave to rise at room temperature for 1 hour, or until it has doubled in size. Once risen, chill in the refrigerator for 30 minutes to make the dough easier to handle.

5   Meanwhile, make the caramel according to the instructions on page 24, then pour it over the bottom of the prepared tin and chill in the refrigerator.

6   Roll the chilled and risen dough out on a floured surface to 25 x 30 cm (10 x 12 in).

Continued Overleaf

PASTRIES   107

7. For the filling, mix together the light brown sugar, cinnamon and cornflour in a small bowl until fully combined. Mix in the butter then spread this over the rolled-out dough. Tightly roll up the dough from the short end.

8. Remove the tin from the refrigerator and arrange the banana slices over the caramel. Cut the dough into six rolls and place on top evenly spread out. Cover with cling film and leave to prove at room temperature for 30 minutes.

9. Preheat the oven to 170°C fan (375°F). Bake for 25 minutes, or until golden brown.

10. Allow to cool for 5 minutes in the tin, then flip it onto a serving plate and spoon any extra caramel in the tin over the rolls. Enjoy warm on its own or with a scoop of your favourite ice cream, if you fancy.

TIPS

Use floss to cut the dough to prevent squashing the dough and to keep the swirls intact.

If your yeast requires activating, sprinkle it over the warm milk and let it bloom for about 5 minutes. Make sure the milk isn't too hot or you will kill the yeast. The yeast will have a creamy foam appearance when ready.

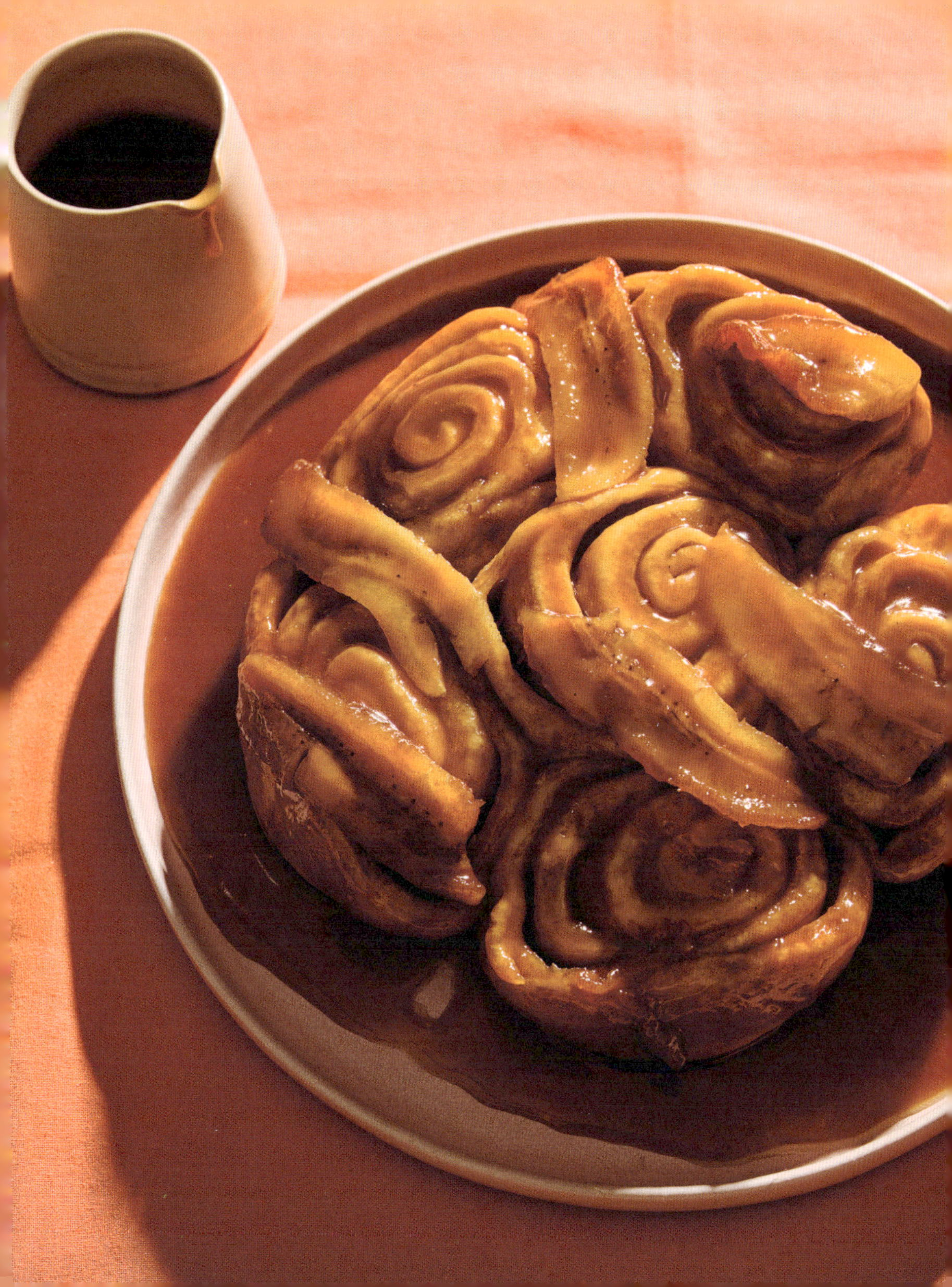

Strawberry & Cream Scones

Makes 6 scones

A classic combination of strawberries and cream but in scone form, which will definitely make you go back for seconds.

---

300 g (10.58 oz) self-raising flour, plus extra for dusting
1 teaspoon baking powder
3 tablespoons caster (superfine) sugar, plus 3 tablespoons for sprinkling
85 g (2.99 oz) cold unsalted butter, cut into cubes
150 g (5.29 oz) milk
100 g (3.52 oz) strawberries, preferably frozen
1 egg, beaten, for egg wash
clotted cream or whipped double (heavy) cream, to serve (optional)

1. Preheat the oven to 170°C fan (375°F) and line a baking tray (pan) with baking parchment.

2. Pulse the flour, baking powder, 3 tablespoons of sugar and butter in a food processor until the mixture is a breadcrumb consistency. Alternatively, add the ingredients to a bowl and, using your fingertips, rub them together until they resemble breadcrumbs. Add the milk and mix until the dough has almost formed, then add the strawberries and mix to incorporate, trying not to break the strawberries up too much.

3. Tip the dough out onto a floured work surface and gather it together into a ball. Flatten the dough, keeping its circular shape as much as possible until you have a rough 20 cm (8 in) circle with a thickness of 6 cm (2½ in). Cut the dough into six triangles or wedges and arrange them on the prepared baking tray. Brush the egg over the scones, including the sides, and sprinkle with the remaining 3 tablespoons of sugar.

4. Bake for 25 minutes, or until golden brown, then allow to cool. Enjoy them on their own or with clotted or whipped cream.

TIP
If you don't have a food processor don't cut your butter but use a grater to make the butter easier to incorporate.

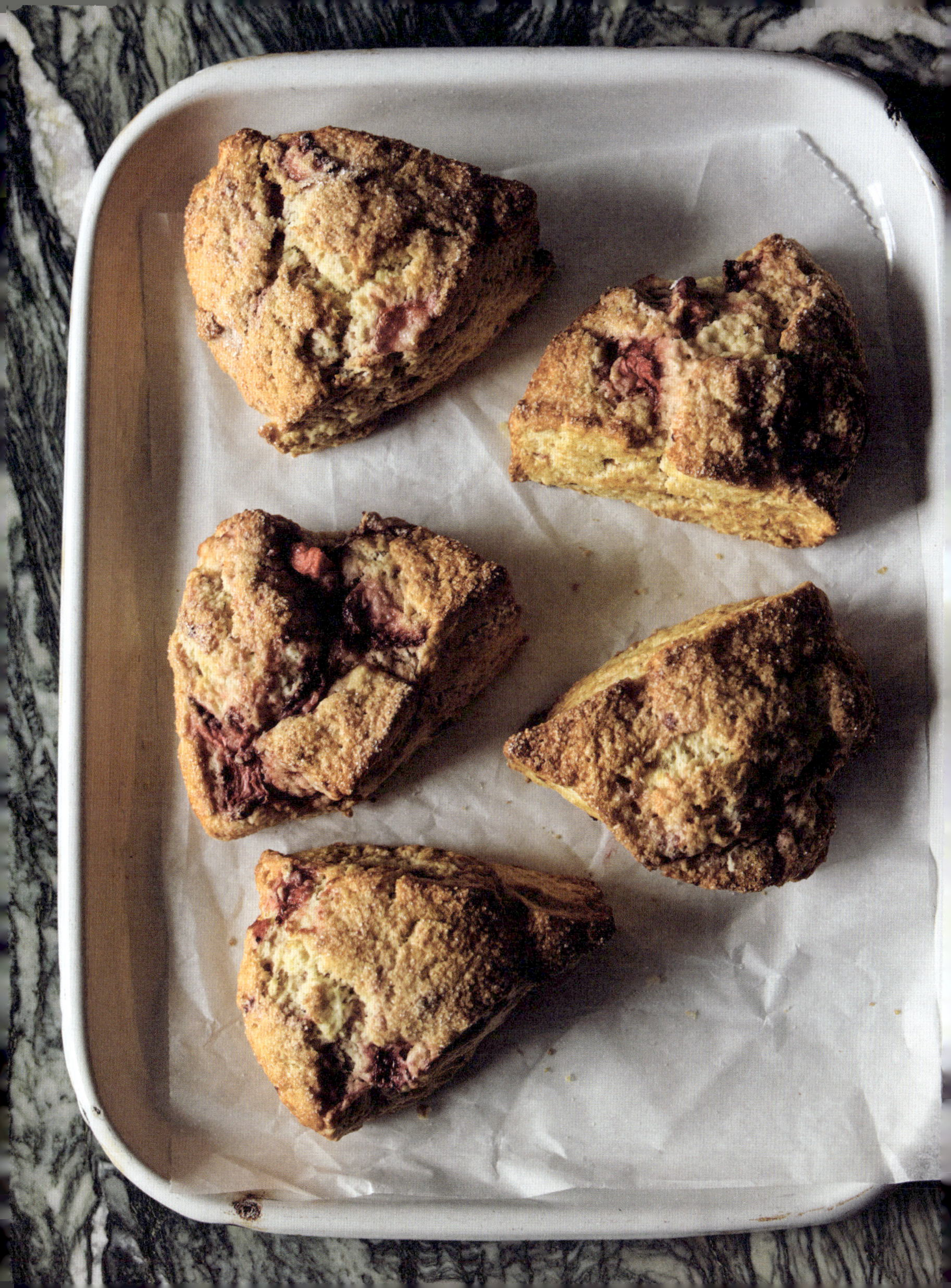

Plum & Rose Craquelin Choux Buns

Makes 8 choux buns

These choux buns have a craquelin biscuit crumb, which makes them bake evenly and gives a them a crunchy texture. Filled with sweet rose cream and plum compote, this makes for a delicious fruity dessert.

For the craquelin

85 g (2.99 oz) unsalted butter, cut into cubes
100 g (3.52 oz) light brown sugar
100 g (3.52 oz) plain (all-purpose) flour

For the choux pastry

125 g (4.40 oz) water
½ teaspoon salt
1 teaspoon caster (superfine) sugar
45 g (1.58 oz) unsalted butter, cut into small chunks
70 g (2.46 oz) plain (all-purpose) flour
2 large eggs, at room temperature

For the plum compote

4 plums, halved, stoned and cut into cubes
40 g (1.41 oz) caster (superfine) sugar
10 g (0.35 oz) lemon juice

For the filling

200 g (7.05 oz) double (heavy) cream
50 g (1.76 oz) icing (confectioners') sugar
1 teaspoon rosewater

To decorate

icing (confectioners') sugar, for dusting
rose petals

TIP

Make sure your dough has cooled before adding the eggs or your mixture could end up runny and hard to use.

1. Preheat the oven to 180°C fan (400°F) and line a baking tray with baking parchment.

2. To make the craquelin, combine the butter, light brown sugar and flour together in a large bowl with a wooden spoon until everything is incorporated. Roll the mixture between two sheets of baking parchment to the thickness of 5 mm (¼ in), then chill in the refrigerator for 30 minutes to harden.

3. For the choux pastry, in a saucepan, heat the water, salt, sugar and butter over a medium heat until the butter is melted. Remove from the heat and add the flour all at once. Return to the heat and stir constantly until the mixture is smooth and pulls away from the sides of the pan, leaving you with a clean pan.

4. Tip the dough into a heatproof bowl and allow to cool for 5 minutes. You can whisk it to cool it down quicker, if you like. Whisk in the eggs, one at a time, until the mixture is smooth and shiny mixture.

5. You can scoop the dough using two spoons or put the dough into a piping bag and pipe it into 7.5 cm (3 in) circles. Arrange them on the prepared baking tray, evenly spaced apart as they will spread when baked. Cut a disc a little bigger than your piped choux, about 9 cm (3½ in) from the chilled craquelin sheet and arrange on top of each choux.

6. Bake for 20 minutes, then reduce the oven temperature to 160°C fan (350°F) and bake for a further 20 minutes to ensure the insides are cooked.

7. Meanwhile, make the plum compote by adding the plums, caster sugar and lemon juice to a pan. Bring to the boil and cook for 10 minutes, then remove from the heat and allow to cool completely.

8. To make the filling, using a hand whisk, whip the cream, icing sugar and rosewater together in a large bowl until soft peaks form.

9. Allow the choux buns to cool completely on the baking tray before cutting them horizontally towards the top. Fill the choux buns with the rose cream, then drizzle the plum compote over and replace the choux 'lids'. Dust with some icing sugar and decorate with rose petals.

Vanilla & Caramelised White Chocolate Churros

Serves 4 (about 16 churro bites)

These churros are bite-sized so can be easily dipped into the white chocolate ganache. You can also replace the caramelised white chocolate ganache with another of your choice. The dough is pretty much the same as the choux buns on page 112, but they have a little less egg so they hold their shape when frying.

For the caramelised white chocolate ganache

- 100 g (3.52 oz) Caramelised White Chocolate (page 23)
- 75 g (2.64 oz) double (heavy) cream

For the vanilla sugar

- 250 g (8.81 oz) caster (superfine) sugar
- 3 tablespoons vanilla bean paste

For the choux pastry

- 125 g (4.40 oz) water
- ½ teaspoon salt
- 1 teaspoon sugar
- 45 g (1.58 oz) unsalted butter, cut into small chunks
- 70 g (2.46 oz) plain (all-purpose) flour
- 1 egg
- 300 g (10.58 oz) vegetable or another flavourless oil, for frying

TIP

Make sure your dough has cooled before adding the eggs or your mixture could end up runny.

1. To make the ganache, melt the caramelised white chocolate and cream together in a heatproof bowl in the microwave for 1 minute, or until fully melted. Stir and set aside.

2. To make the vanilla sugar, mix the caster sugar and vanilla together in a large bowl until combined. Set aside.

3. Line a baking tray with baking parchment and set aside. For the choux pastry, in a saucepan, heat the water, salt, sugar and butter together until the butter is melted. Remove from the heat and add the flour all at once. Return to the heat and stir constantly until the mixture is smooth and pulls away from the sides of the pan, leaving you with a clean pan.

4. Tip the dough into a heatproof bowl and allow to cool for 2 minutes. You can whisk it to cool it down quicker, if you like. Whisk in the egg until the mixture is smooth and shiny, then spoon it into a piping bag with an open star nozzle (page 40). Pipe 5 cm (2 in) long churros onto the prepared baking tray. Once all the dough has been piped, place in the freezer until completely frozen.

5. When you are ready to fry your churros, heat the oil in a large, deep saucepan and test it's ready by dipping a wooden spoon into the oil. If small bubbles form it's ready. Carefully add the churros to the hot oil and fry for 3–4 minutes until golden brown then place on a baking tray lined with paper towels to drain the excess oil. You may need to fry in batches as too many in the pan at once will slow down the cooking process and result in oily churros. While still warm, toss the churros in the vanilla sugar and enjoy with the ganache. They are best eaten the same day.

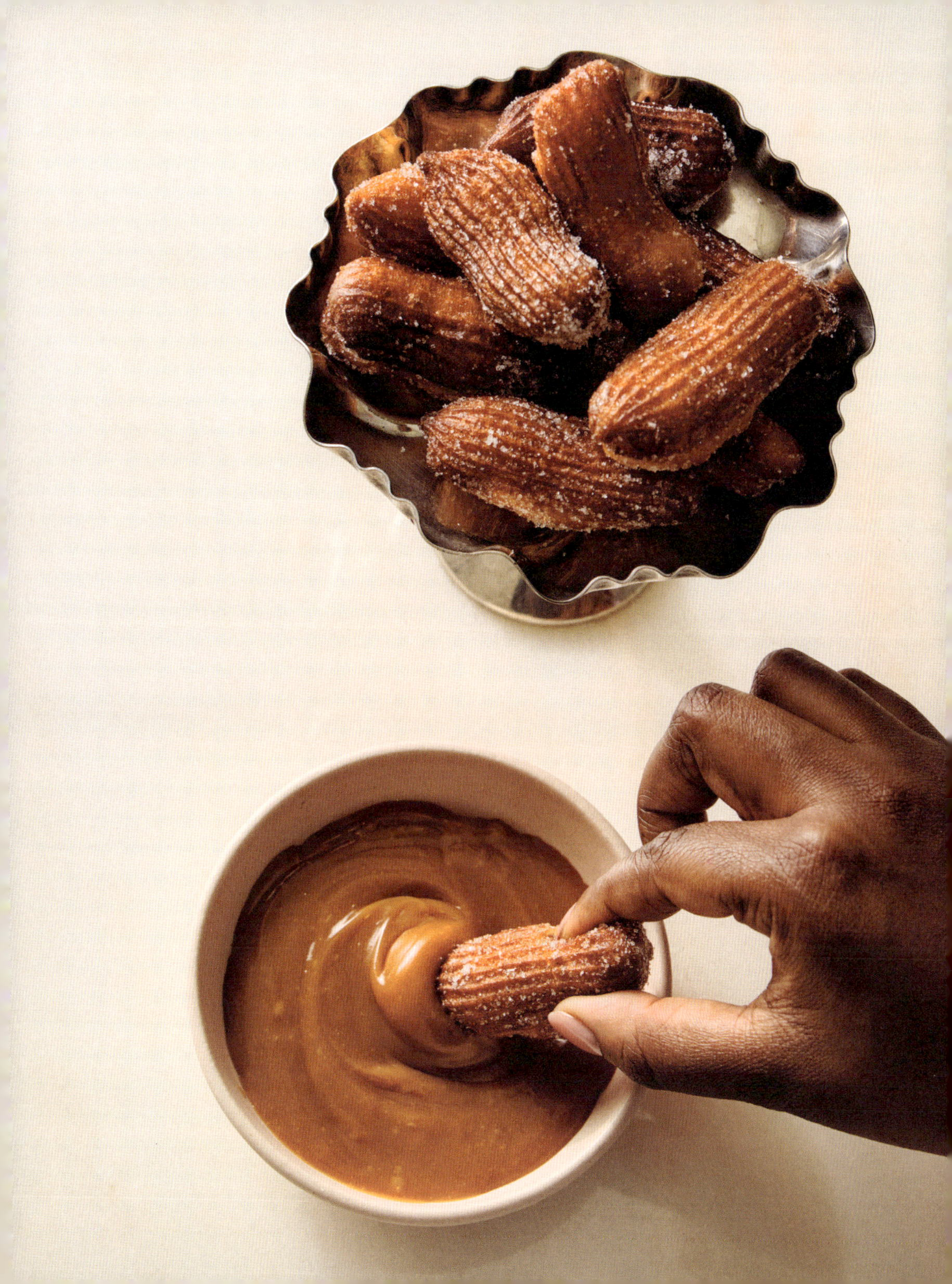

Raspberry Custard Buns

Makes 5–6 buns

These light and fluffy brioche-style buns with a baked raspberry custard are perfect for a quick homemade baked pastry.

For the filling

300 g (10.58 oz) Custard (page 29)
25 g (0.88 oz) fresh raspberries

For the dough

flavourless oil, such as vegetable oil
1 teaspoon fast-action dried yeast
150 g (5.29 oz) strong white flour, plus extra for dusting
15 g (0.52 oz) caster (superfine) sugar
¼ teaspoon salt
100 g (3.52 oz) whole milk, at room temperature
15 g (0.52 oz) unsalted butter, softened and cut into cubes
1 egg, beaten, for egg wash

To decorate

1 egg, beaten, for egg wash
2 tablespoons sugar pearls
25 g (0.88 oz) freeze-dried raspberries
icing (confectioners') sugar, for dusting

1. Make the custard for the filling according to the instructions on page 29 with the addition of the raspberries and set aside to cool in the refrigerator.

2. For the dough, line a large baking tray with baking parchment and lightly oil a large bowl and set aside. Add the yeast, flour, caster sugar and salt to a large bowl and mix to combine. Add the milk and mix until a dough starts to form, then mix or knead until you have a smooth dough. I recommend doing this in a stand mixer fitted with a dough hook attachment to speed up the process, but you can also knead the dough on a lightly floured work surface.

3. Once the dough is smooth, add the softened butter, a cube at a time, until it is all incorporated and the dough is no longer sticky and has a nice stretch to it. Leave to rise in the oiled bowl for 1 hour at room temperature, or until doubled in size.

4. Once the dough has risen, tip it out onto a lightly floured surface, then chop into six pieces and roll into balls. Leave them to rest at room temperature for about 15 minutes.

5. Arrange the balls on the prepared baking tray, spaced apart as they will expand during baking. Using a damp spoon, create a dip in the centre of each ball. Spoon the custard into a piping bag then pipe it into the centre of the dough, or use a spoon. Leave to prove at room temperature for 30 minutes.

6. Preheat the oven to 170°C fan (375°F). Once the dough has risen, brush with the egg, sprinkle with the sugar pearls and add the raspberries. Bake for 20–25 minutes until golden brown and springy to the touch. Remove from the oven and finish with a dusting of icing sugar. They are best eaten the same day.

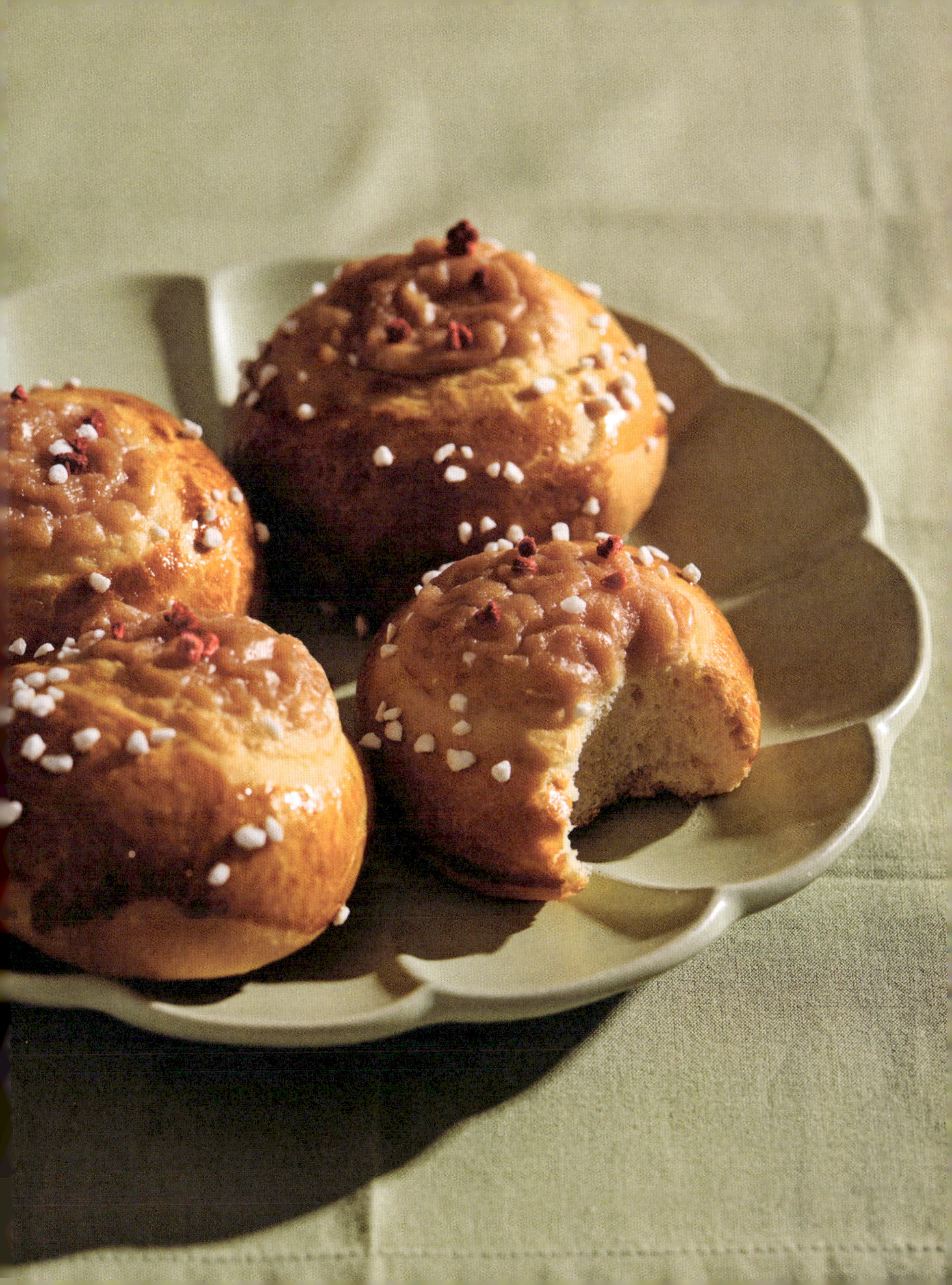

ABOUT THE AUTHOR

Dee Omole is a London-based pastry chef, food stylist and the founder of Dee's Basement, a dessert studio known for its playful, nostalgic and beautifully designed bakes. What started as a passion for creating sweet treats quickly turned into a thriving business, with her signature hand-painted chocolate-covered madeleines and fun bento cakes gaining a loyal following.

Dee's love for baking is all about blending creativity with flavour and making desserts that taste just as incredible as they look. Her work has been featured in publications, such as the *Evening Standard*, and she's built a strong online community of fellow dessert lovers. Her unique confections blend creativity with precision, offering not just desserts but edible art.

In her debut baking book, Dee shares her expertise, inspiration and recipes, inviting readers to explore her world of vibrant flavours and stunning designs. Whether you're a novice or a seasoned baker, Dee's guidance will empower you to create confections that are as delightful to the eye as they are to the palate. Whether you're a beginner or a pro, she hopes to bring a little extra joy (and sugar) into your kitchen.

When she's not baking, Dee is probably experimenting with new flavours, styling her latest creations, or hunting down the best pastries in town. You can find her on socials @deesbasement and @deeomole.

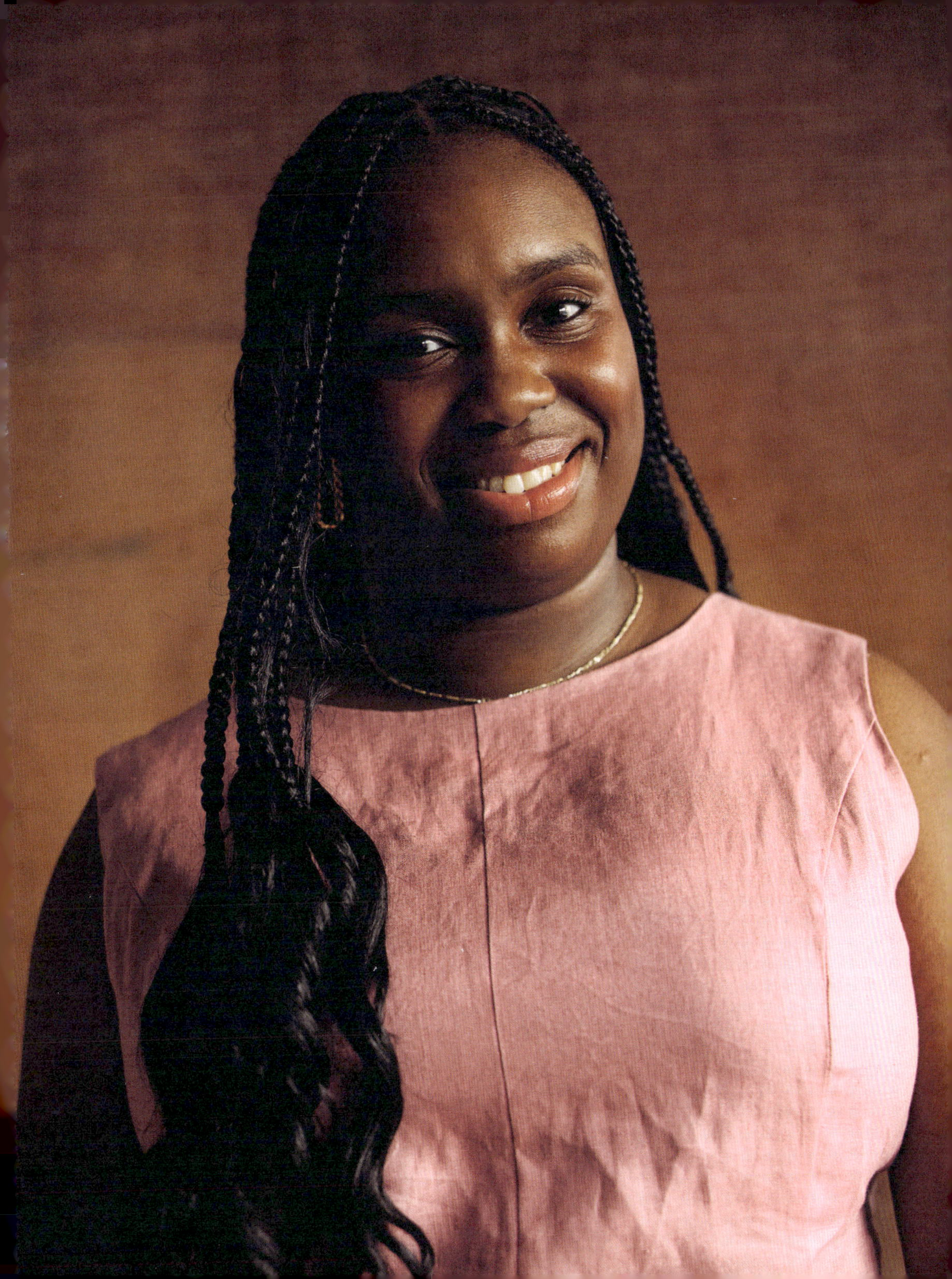

ACKNOWLEDGEMENTS

Writing this book has been a journey but an incredibly fulfilling one and I couldn't have done it without the love and support of so many incredible people.

First and foremost, thank you, God, for the continuous blessings I have received over the years, and for blessing me with the ability and skills to do this for a living.

My family for their unwavering support through everything, for being my guinea pigs and helping me through messes both physically and emotionally. Mum and Dad, thank you for being amazing parents who always encouraged my sisters and me to pursue anything we wanted to do, telling us anything is possible and not having to take the traditional career path and providing us with protection both physically and spiritually. Mum, thank you for being the one who first introduced me to baking. Those moments in the kitchen with you baking and cooking were where my love for this craft truly began. Dad, thank you for your endless advice and guidance both in business and spiritually, and thank you for being an unofficial employee all these years, helping me to navigate the world of business and entrepreneurship and for giving me advice on all things business especially when I didn't have a clue what I was doing. The encouragement, patience and endless belief you both have had in me has shaped the baker (and person) I am today. Thank you to my sisters, Abi, Jay and Lolade. You guys are my best friends. I am so incredibly thankful to have you guys and the close relationship we have. You guys always support everything I do but also aren't afraid to tell me when an idea I have is interesting. Thanks for being a soundboard but also for cheering me on in everything I do. Thank you to my Aunty Nikky who is always willing to help out no matter the job or task without complaining (most times, haha). To my Grandparents, who I miss dearly. I know you would be proud of what I've done with my career and what is to come. Also, a big thank you to the rest of my family, uncles, aunties and cousins, as well as family friends, back home in Nigeria, in the UK, in the US and everywhere in between.

To my friends: you know who you are! From helping out with markets and pop ups, being some of my first customers in the early days whilst I was still developing my skills, celebrating milestones with me and always encouraging me to pursue my business back in secondary school or university, thank you! You guys provided me with motivation and encouragement in the early days that kept me going.

To my fellow chefs, stylists and the creators in industry, who have become friends. Thank you for late-night brainstorming or venting sessions, honest feedback, and shared passion for food, which has been invaluable. I'm so grateful to be surrounded by such talented and inspiring people who are so collaborative and encouraging.

A big thank you to Hardie Grant for making this all possible. Thank you to Kajal, for reaching out regarding publishing a book and to Eila and the rest of the Hardie Grant team, for answering my endless questions and emails. Thank you to Matt and Ruth, for the lovely photography and bringing great vibes throughout the shoot days; Beth and the Nic & Lou team, for the beautiful designs and editing; Alice for being the best stylist anyone could ask for and making shoot days feel effortless; and Sean, for being an extra set of much needed helping hands.

To everyone who has supported Dee's Basement – whether you've ordered a cake, shared a post, or just sent me a kind message – you've been such a huge part of this journey. This book is for you as much as it is for me and it wouldn't exist without you. And finally, to anyone who picks up this book: I hope these recipes bring as much joy to your kitchen as they've brought to mine. Baking is about more than just the end result: it's about the love, creativity and memories you make along the way. Keep creating, keep experimenting, and most importantly, have fun!

With love and gratitude,

Dee x

JAMES 1:17

"Every good and perfect gift is from above, coming down from the Father of the heavenly lights, who does not change like shifting shadows."

INDEX

A

almonds
   cherry Bakewell tart 106
   olive oil & orange loaf cake 60
   peach & cardamom galette 102
   raspberry & orange blossom friand 48
American buttercream 20
apple cinnamon crumb cake 50

B

bananas
   madeleines banana pudding 84
   salted caramel banana bread 57
   upside-down banoffee roll 107–8
bay leaf
   strawberry & bay leaf jam biscuit sandwich 66
biscuits. see cookies & biscuits
Black Forest tiramisu 92
blackberries
   Earl Grey & blackberry coulis blancmange 96
blancmange
   Earl Grey & blackberry coulis blancmange 96
blondies
   birthday cake blondies 87
blueberries
   lemon & blueberry crumble cookies 71
brown butter 26
   brown butter pumpkin spice deep dish cookies 70
   chocolate cake with brown butter cream cheese frosting 54
   salted caramel banana bread 57
brownies
   brownie s'mores cookies 75
   brownie with espresso whipped cream 86
butter. see brown butter
buttercream
   American buttercream 20
   buttercream dams 39
   chocolate buttercream 19
   coconut buttercream 19
   cookies 'n' cream buttercream 19
   Italian meringue buttercream 18
   lemon buttercream 19
   mock 'meringue' buttercream 21
   piping techniques/styles 40
   salted caramel buttercream 19

C

cakes
   apple cinnamon crumb cake 50
   birthday cake blondies 87
   brownie with espresso whipped cream 86
   chocolate cake with brown butter cream cheese frosting 54
   chocolate-covered cherry madeleines 46
   chocolate-covered edible flower madeleines 47
   Matcha & strawberry Swiss roll cake 52
   olive oil & orange loaf cake 60
   raspberry & orange blossom friand 48
   raspberry Eton mess mini cakes 58

salted caramel banana bread 57
vanilla cake 36–7
vanilla madeleines 42
caramelised white chocolate 23
   brown butter pumpkin spice deep dish cookies 70
   chocolate & caramelised white chocolate cookies 74
   vanilla & caramelised white chocolate churros 114
cardamom
   peach & cardamom galette 102
cherries
   Black Forest tiramisu 92
   cherry Bakewell tart 106
   chocolate-covered cherry madeleines 46
chocolate
   birthday cake blondies 87
   Black Forest tiramisu 92
   brown butter pumpkin spice deep dish cookies 70
   brownie s'mores cookies 75
   brownie with espresso whipped cream 86
   caramelised white chocolate 23
   chocolate & caramelised white chocolate cookies 74
   chocolate buttercream 19
   chocolate cake 36–7
   chocolate cake with brown butter cream cheese frosting 54
   chocolate-covered cherry madeleines 46
   chocolate-covered edible flower madeleines 47
   ganache 22

   melting chocolate 43
   vanilla & caramelised white chocolate churros 114
   white chocolate and raspberry cake 36–7
choux pastry
   plum & rose craquelin choux buns 112–13
churros
   vanilla & caramelised white chocolate churros 114
cinnamon
   apple cinnamon crumb cake 50
   brown butter pumpkin spice deep dish cookies 70
   upside-down banoffee roll 107–8
coconut
   coconut and lime cake 36–7
   coconut buttercream 19
coffee
   brownie with espresso whipped cream 86
cookies & biscuits 30
   brown butter pumpkin spice deep dish cookies 70
   brownie s'mores cookies 75
   chocolate & caramelised white chocolate cookies 74
   lavender shortbread 76
   lemon & blueberry crumble cookies 71
   raspberry checkerboard biscuits 68
   strawberry & bay leaf jam biscuit sandwich 66
cookies 'n' cream
   cookies 'n' cream buttercream 19
   cookies 'n' cream cake 36–7

couplers 39
craquelin
   plum & rose craquelin choux buns 112–13
cream
   Black Forest tiramisu 92
   brown butter pumpkin spice deep dish cookies 70
   brownie with espresso whipped cream 86
   crème brûlée Basque cheesecake 90–1
   ganache 22
   madeleines banana pudding 84
   mango & lemon Pavlova 82
   Matcha & strawberry Swiss roll cake 52
   plum & rose craquelin choux buns 112–13
   raspberry & pistachio trifle 94
   raspberry Eton mess mini cakes 58
   salted caramel 24
   strawberry & cream scones 110
   upside-down banoffee roll 107–8
   vanilla & caramelised white chocolate churros 114
cream cheese
   chocolate cake with brown butter cream cheese frosting 54
   cream cheese frosting 20
   crème brûlée Basque cheesecake 90–1
   red velvet cake 36–7
crème brûlée Basque cheesecake 90–1
crumb coating cakes 39
crumble topping
   apple cinnamon crumb cake 50
   lemon & blueberry crumble cookies 71

custard 29
   crème brûlée Basque cheesecake 90–1
   madeleines banana pudding 84
   raspberry custard buns 116

D

desserts
   birthday cake blondies 87
   Black Forest tiramisu 92
   brownie with espresso whipped cream 86
   cherry Bakewell tart 106
   crème brûlée Basque cheesecake 90–1
   Earl Grey & blackberry coulis blancmange 96
   madeleines banana pudding 84
   mango & lemon Pavlova 82
   mango & lime tarts 104
   peach & cardamom galette 102
   raspberry & pistachio trifle 94

E

Earl Grey & blackberry coulis blancmange 96
eggs
   crème brûlée Basque cheesecake 90–1
   custard 29
   Italian meringue buttercream 18
   lemon curd 28
   madeleines banana pudding 84
   mango & lemon Pavlova 82
   raspberry Eton mess mini cakes 58
equipment 10–11

F

flowers, edible
   chocolate-covered edible flower
      madeleines 47
frangipane
   cherry Bakewell tart 106
   peach & cardamom galette 102
friands
   raspberry & orange blossom friand 48

G

galettes
   peach & cardamom galette 102
ganache 22
   vanilla & caramelised white chocolate
      churros 114
   white chocolate and raspberry cake 36–7
gingerbread biscuits 30

I

icing/toppings
   American buttercream 20
   caramelised white chocolate 23
   chocolate buttercream 19
   coconut buttercream 19
   cookies 'n' cream buttercream 19
   cream cheese frosting 20
   ganache 22
   Italian meringue buttercream 18
   lemon buttercream 19
   mock 'meringue' buttercream 21
   piping bags 39

   salted caramel 24
   salted caramel buttercream 19
   sugar syrup 25
Italian meringue buttercream 18

J

jam
   strawberry jam 27

L

lavender shortbread 76
lemons
   lemon & blueberry crumble cookies 71
   lemon buttercream 19
   lemon cake 36–7
   lemon curd 28
   mango & lemon Pavlova 82
limes
   coconut and lime cake 36–7
   mango & lime tarts 104

M

madeleines
   chocolate-covered cherry madeleines 46
   chocolate-covered edible flower
      madeleines 47
   madeleines banana pudding 84
   vanilla madeleines 42
mangos
   mango & lemon Pavlova 82
   mango & lime tarts 104

marshmallows
   brownie s'mores cookies 75
mascarpone
   Black Forest tiramisu 92
Matcha & strawberry Swiss roll cake 52
meringues
   mango & lemon Pavlova 82
   raspberry Eton mess mini cakes 58
milk
   crème brûlée Basque cheesecake 90–1
   custard 29
   Earl Grey & blackberry coulis
      blancmange 96
   madeleines banana pudding 84
mock 'meringue' buttercream 21

O

olive oil & orange loaf cake 60
orange blossom water
   raspberry & orange blossom friand 48
oranges
   olive oil & orange loaf cake 60

P

pastries
   cherry Bakewell tart 106
   mango & lime tarts 104
   peach & cardamom galette 102
   plum & rose craquelin choux buns
      112–13
   raspberry custard buns 116
   strawberry & cream scones 110

upside-down banoffee roll 107–8
vanilla & caramelised white chocolate
   churros 114
pastry
   choux pastry 112–13
   shortcrust pastry 31
peach & cardamom galette 102
piping bags 39
piping techniques/styles 40
pistachios
   raspberry & pistachio trifle 94
plum & rose craquelin choux buns 112–13
pumpkin
   brown butter pumpkin spice deep dish
      cookies 70
pumpkin spice blend
   brown butter pumpkin spice deep dish
      cookies 70

R

raspberries
   raspberry & orange blossom friand 48
   raspberry & pistachio trifle 94
   raspberry custard buns 116
   raspberry Eton mess mini cakes 58
   white chocolate and raspberry cake 36–7
raspberry jam
   raspberry Eton mess mini cakes 58
raspberry powder
   raspberry checkerboard biscuits 68
red velvet cake 36–7
rosewater
   plum & rose craquelin choux buns
      112–13

S

salted caramel 24
  salted caramel banana bread 57
  salted caramel buttercream 19
  salted caramel cake 36–7
scones
  strawberry & cream scones 110
shortbread
  lavender shortbread 76
shortcrust pastry 31
strawberries
  strawberry & cream scones 110
  strawberry jam 27
strawberry jam 27
  Matcha & strawberry Swiss roll cake 52
  strawberry & bay leaf jam biscuit
    sandwich 66
sugar syrup 25
Swiss roll
  Matcha & strawberry Swiss roll cake 52

T

tiramisu
  Black Forest tiramisu 92
trifles
  raspberry & pistachio trifle 94

U

upside-down banoffee roll 107–8

V

vanilla & caramelised white chocolate churros 114
vanilla cake 36–7
vanilla madeleines 42

Quadrille, Penguin Random House UK, One Embassy Gardens, 8 Viaduct Gardens, London SW11 7BW

Quadrille Publishing Limited is part of the Penguin Random House group of companies whose addresses can be found at global.penguinrandomhouse.com

Penguin Random House UK

Text © Adeola Omole 2025
Illustrations © Beth Free, Studio Nic&Lou 2025

Dee Omole has asserted her right to be identified as the author of this Work in accordance with the Copyright, Designs and Patents Act 1988

Penguin Random House values and supports copyright. Copyright fuels creativity, encourages diverse voices, promotes freedom of expression and supports a vibrant culture. Thank you for purchasing an authorised edition of this book and for respecting intellectual property laws by not reproducing, scanning or distributing any part of it by any means without permission. You are supporting authors and enabling Penguin Random House to continue to publish books for everyone. No part of this book may be used or reproduced in any manner for the purpose of training artificial intelligence technologies or systems. In accordance with Article 4(3) of the DSM Directive 2019/790, Penguin Random House expressly reserves this work from the text and data mining exception.

Published by Quadrille in 2025

www.penguin.co.uk

A CIP catalogue record for this book is available from the British Library

ISBN 978-1-83783-363-4
10 9 8 7 6 5 4 3 2 1

Managing Director, Publishing: Sarah Lavelle
Publishing Director: Kajal Mistry
Senior Editor: Eila Purvis
Designer: Beth Free, Studio Nic&Lou
Photographer: Matt Russell
Copy-editor: Katy Steer
Proofreader: Lorraine Jerram
Indexer: Cathy Heath
Props Stylist: Hannah Wilkinson
Food Stylist: Alice Katie Hughes
Production Manager: Sabeena Atchia

Colour reproduction by F1

Printed in China by RR Donnelley Asia Printing Solution Limited

The authorised representative in the EEA is Penguin Random House Ireland, Morrison Chambers, 32 Nassau Street, Dublin D02 YH68.

MIX
Paper from responsible sources
FSC® C018179